A Government as Good as Its People

by Jimmy Carter

SIMON AND SCHUSTER

NEW YORK

Designed by Irving Perkins
Manufactured in the United States of America

1 2 3 4 5 6 7 8 9 10

Library of Congress Cataloging in Publication Data

Carter, Jimmy, 1924–
A government as good as its people.

1. United States—Politics and government—1974–
1977—Collected works. 2. United States—Politics
and government—1977–   —Collected works.
3. Georgia—Politics and government—1951–   —
Collected works. 4. Carter, Jimmy, 1924–
I. Title.
E838.5.C375   1977   309.1'73'0925   77-2641
ISBN 0-671-22815-3

Contents

3. Toward the Presidency/July–November 1976

4. Inaugural Address/January 20, 1977

Introduction

by Jimmy Carter

A MEMBER of my staff once calculated that I delivered 1,200 speeches as Governor of Georgia and another 2,100 speeches during my Presidential campaign—in all, a great many speeches by anyone's standard.

This volume collects all or part of about fifty of those speeches, with emphasis on those delivered during my Presidential campaign.

We have tried, in editing this book, not to provide a formal collection of "major" speeches but to try to suggest the variety of ways in which I, as a candidate, presented myself to the American people. Thus we have included not only formal speeches on specific issues but informal remarks to political gatherings, as well as news conferences, interviews, and excerpts from my debates with President Ford.

I hope this collection will reflect what is to me a basic truth about Presidential politics—that one does not pursue the Presidency by high oratory but by plain talk, not by talking down to people but simply by talking to people, directly and candidly.

As I ran for President, my most basic means of communication was what we called the "stump speeches"—the informal remarks I made to hundreds of political receptions and rallies, setting out the personal beliefs and political themes upon which my candidacy was based. These short speeches were almost invariably followed by a cross-examination type of question period.

7

I said certain things over and over, day after day, month after month. That government can be both competent and compassionate. That America's foreign policy should reflect the character of the American people. That we could have, and must have, a government as good as its people.

Reporters who traveled with us sometimes complained that they were tired of hearing those same few speeches again and again. It was an understandable complaint, at least from their perspective, but I was not speaking for the entertainment of the press corps.

I was speaking, each time, to people who had never before seen me in person and who might never see me again. I wanted them to remember me. I wanted them to support me. And I wanted them to judge me on an informed basis, on the basis of my most deeply held beliefs as I had come to express them in those basic stump speeches.

Those few speeches evolved over the months, of course, and in this volume we have included examples of various stages of their development. But I believe the reader will find that my basic message was very much the same during the final weeks of my campaign, when I was addressing thousands of people at huge outdoor rallies, as it was in the early weeks, when I was talking to a handful of people in someone's living room.

Inevitably, as the campaign progressed, I began to give more prepared speeches on specific issues. Often, major organizations would invite me to appear before them with the hope that I would address issues of special importance to them. Thus, I spoke on foreign policy to the Foreign Policy Association in June of 1976, on urban policy to the Conference of Mayors later that month, on defense policy to the American Legion in August, on human rights to B'nai B'rith in September, on family policy to the National Conference of Catholic Charities in October, and so on.

These speeches, too, were an important part of the campaign—detailed statements of my views on specific issues before informed, sometimes critical, audiences, with major media coverage and analysis. In preparing such speeches, it was necessary to confront hard issues directly; when I went before the American Legion, for example, I knew that many of its members would not approve of my plan to pardon draft evaders, but I felt an obligation to meet the issue head-on before one of the groups most concerned about it. Some of the Legion members booed when I stated my position, but I felt that was less important than that they, and the American people, should know exactly where I stood.

In the interest of providing as broad a picture as possible of the campaign, we have given only excerpts of most of the speeches collected here. The ones that are presented in their entirety (or with only minor editing) are the Georgia Inaugural, the remarks at the unveiling of the Martin Luther King portrait, the impromptu Law Day speech, the remarks at the Martin Luther King Hospital in Los Angeles, the Acceptance speech at Madison Square Garden, the Town Hall Forum speech, the Jerry Litton Memorial Dinner speech, the speech to the Conference of Catholic Charities, and the Inaugural Address.

I said many times during the campaign that I hoped to create an intimate, personal relationship between myself and the American people, and my speeches were the primary way I went about building that relationship. To travel about this land, to meet people, to talk to them, to learn from them, to gain their support, was a rare and exhilarating experience, an unforgettable experience, and the finest possible training for the job I sought and now hold.

I hope that this volume can be part of my continuing effort to communicate with the people of America and of all the world. I hope it will make my views known more widely and in greater detail than before. And I intend for it to remind me, and the people who elected me, of the commitments I made as a candidate and the standards to which I must be held accountable as long as I hold the office of President.

1

Governor
of
Georgia

1971–1974

From Plains to Atlanta

IT IS a long way from Plains to Atlanta. I started the trip four and a half years ago, and with a four-year detour, I finally made it. I thank you all for making it possible for me to be here on what is certainly the greatest day of my life. But now the election is over, and I realize that the test of a leader is not how well he campaigned but how effectively he meets the challenges and responsibilities of the office.

Our country was founded on the premise that government continually derives its power from independent and free men and women. If it is to survive, confident and courageous citizens must be willing to assume responsibility for the quality of our government at any particular time in history.

This is a time for truth and frankness. The next four years will not be easy ones. The problems we face will not solve themselves. They demand the utmost in dedication and unselfishness from each of us. But this is also a time for greatness. Our people are determined to overcome the handicaps of the past and to meet the opportunities of the future with confidence and with courage.

Our people are our most precious possession and we cannot afford to waste the talents and abilities given by God to one single Georgian. Every adult illiterate, every school dropout, every untrained retarded child is an indictment of us all. Our state pays a terrible and continuing human and financial price for these failures. It is time to end this waste. If Switzerland and Israel and other people can eliminate illiteracy, then so can we.

The responsibility is our own, and as Governor, I will not shirk this responsibility.

At the end of a long campaign, I believe I know our people

13

as well as anyone. Based on this knowledge of Georgians—north and south, rural and urban, liberal and conservative—I say to you quite frankly that the time for racial discrimination is over. Our people have already made this major and difficult decision, but we cannot underestimate the challenge of hundreds of minor decisions yet to be made. Our inherent human charity and our religious beliefs will be taxed to the limit.

No poor, rural, weak, or black person should ever again have to bear the additional burden of being deprived of the opportunity for an education, a job, or simple justice. We Georgians are fully capable of making our own judgments and managing our own affairs.

We who are strong or in positions of leadership must realize that the responsibility for making correct decisions in the future is ours. As Governor, I will never shirk this responsibility.

Georgia is a state of great natural beauty and promise, but the quality of our natural surroundings is threatened because of avarice, selfishness, procrastination, and neglect. Change and development are necessary for the growth of our population and for the progress of our agricultural, recreational, and industrial life. Our challenge is to insure that such activities avoid destruction and dereliction of our environment.

The responsibility for meeting this challenge is our own. As Governor, I will not shirk this responsibility.

In Georgia we are determined that the law shall be enforced. Peace officers must have our appreciation and complete support. We cannot educate a child, build a highway, equalize tax burdens, create harmony among our people, or preserve basic human freedom unless we have an orderly society.

Crime and lack of justice are especially cruel to those who are least able to protect themselves. Swift arrest and trial and fair punishment should be expected by those who would break our laws. It is equally important to us that every effort be made to rehabilitate lawbreakers into useful and productive members of society. We have not yet attained these goals in Georgia, but now we must.

The proper function of a government is to make it easy for people to do good and difficult for them to do evil. This responsibility is our own. I will not shirk this responsibility.

Like thousands of other businessmen in Georgia, I have always attempted to conduct my business in an honest and efficient manner. Like thousands of other citizens, I expect no less of government.

The functions of government should be administered so as to justify confidence and pride.

Taxes should be minimal and fair.

Rural and urban people should easily discern the mutuality of their goals and opportunities.

We should make our major investments in people, not buildings.

With wisdom and judgment we should take future actions according to carefully considered long-range plans and priorities.

Governments closest to the people should be strengthened, and the efforts of our local, state, and national governments need to be thoroughly coordinated.

We should remember that our state can best be served by a strong and independent governor, working with a strong and independent legislature.

Government is a contrivance of human wisdom to provide for human wants. People have a right to expect that these wants will be provided for by this wisdom.

The test of a government is not how popular it is with the powerful and privileged few but how honestly and fairly it deals with the many who must depend upon it.

William Jennings Bryan said, "Destiny is not a matter of

chance, it is a matter of choice. Destiny is not a thing to be waited for, it is a thing to be achieved."

Here around me are seated the members of the Georgia Legislature and other state officials. They are dedicated and honest men and women. They love this state as you love it and I love it. But no group of elected officers, no matter how dedicated and enlightened, can control the destiny of a great state like ours. What officials can solve alone the problems of crime, welfare, illiteracy, disease, injustice, pollution, and waste? This control rests in your hands, the people of Georgia.

In a democracy, no government can be stronger or wiser or more just than its people. The idealism of the college student, the compassion of a mother, the common sense of the businessman, the time and experience of a retired couple, and the vision of political leaders must all be harnessed to bring out the best in our state.

As I have said many times during the last few years, I am determined that at the end of this administration we shall be able to stand up anywhere in the world—in New York, California, or Florida—and say, "I'm a Georgian," and be proud of it.

I welcome the challenge and the opportunity of serving as Governor of our state during the next four years. I promise you my best. I ask you for your best.

Inauguration Address
Atlanta, Georgia
January 12, 1971

An Inner Urge

. . . INSTILLED WITHIN me and within your hearts is an acknowledgment sometimes not spoken. There is a mandatory relationship between the powerful and the influential and the socially prominent and wealthy on the one hand, and the weak, the insecure, and the poor on the other hand.

This is a relationship not always completely understood. I don't completely understand it myself. But I know that in a free society we do see very clearly that one cannot accept great blessings bestowed on him by God without feeling an inner urge and drive to share those blessings with others of our neighbors who are not quite so fortunate as we.

Lions' Convention
Jekyll Island, Georgia
June 8, 1971

Things I Want to Change

I'VE GOT a good business and I've got a lot of employees and I make good money and I can see that the functions of a state government and the local governments don't particularly matter to me in a direct way. My children and I and my wife are not on welfare, so except for saving the taxpayers' money I don't really care in a personal way, as far as my own family is concerned, if the Welfare Department does a good job or the Labor Department or Vocational Rehabilitation or Corrections or Pardons and Parole or Probation. Those things don't make any difference much to my own family, nor to the powerful, wealthy people who have always run the state government, but they do have a direct impact and it makes a lot of difference to the ones who are dependent on the state government to make sure that they can overcome handicaps with which they may have been born, either being born in poverty or being born and not having a chance to have a good education or being born on a peanut farm or being born black or being born with a hearing or speech deficiency or maybe deformed in some way.

People deserve every right to take whatever talent they have and develop it, and to have a chance to appreciate themselves and to stand with a degree of human dignity and say, "I'm a man, just like the next fellow, and I have desires and I have needs and I have accomplishments that I can perform and I have talent that God has given me and I want my talents to be developed and used just like the next fellow and I live in a free country, but quite often I haven't been completely free."

That's the kind of need and the kind of frustration that the state government is supposed to meet and I'm trying, through this Goals for Georgia program, to get ideas from different people all over the state, who would tell me, "Governor, I think our state ought to do this and hasn't been doing it." "I've got a retarded child at home and he's been on the waiting list for Gracewood for eight years and I haven't got him in yet," or "I hold a job and I don't think I'm getting an adequate chance to be promoted," or "I have a chance for a better job across town and I can't get over there because it costs too much," or "I'm a mother and my husband is dead and I've got these kids and I don't have a place to keep them during the day so I can support myself," or "I see the State Highway Department paving streets on the nice side of town and the street that goes by my house is not even paved."

Well, those are the kinds of things I want to change and I can't change them by myself, because in a lot of ways I can't look at government with different ideas and different viewpoints; and I want to have a way to get harnessed and put before my eyes as Governor the suggestions on how we can make Georgia's government a better government. We've got a lot of progress that we can make in our state, and I intend to make it.

Goals for Georgia
Kennedy School
Atlanta, Georgia
July 1, 1971

Preserving Georgia

... WE DON'T have any inclination to attract a new industry to Georgia who is dependent upon a special tax break or privilege at the expense of his neighbors who have been here many years. We don't ask you to come here to be a new neighbor of ours if you expect cheap labor. And we don't expect you to come here in Georgia to be a new neighbor if you anticipate any despoiling or derogation of the land or the air or the water within which we must live.

Red Carpet Tour
Macon, Georgia
April 5, 1972

The Women in My Life

. . . SOMEONE ASKED me as I came in if I felt in the minority and I said, "Well, I have felt this way almost all of my life." My mother is a registered nurse, and when we grew up on the farm she was always a dominant factor in our family. After my father's death she became instead of less active, more active, and at the age of sixty-eight she announced to the family that she had just joined the Peace Corps, and she spent two years in India helping Mrs. Gandhi. You might think that she was the most dominant female factor in my life, but that is not true. There's my wife, Rosalynn, whom I married a little more than twenty-five years ago, whom I love more now than I did when I married her, and who helped me in 1970 to personally visit, look in the eye, talk to, meet, and ask for the help of more than six hundred thousand Georgians. And when I went in one direction, early in the morning, she went in a different one, and she visited the factory shift lines, walked in and out of the stores and shopping centers, and worked in a very remarkable way to help me be Governor. You might think that she was the most dominant female factor in my life, but that is not true. After we had been married years and had three ugly boys in our house, we tried again after a fourteen-year argument, which I finally won, and we now have a four-year-old daughter named Amy. And Amy is the female dominant factor in my life.

League of Women Voters
Atlanta, Georgia
May 1, 1972

Unfulfilled Dreams and Crushed Hopes

... THERE ARE unfulfilled dreams and crushed hopes in our society. And one of the major responsibilities of any man or any woman with a major opportunity for public service is to remove those constraints. ...

I know the affliction of a child who goes into the first grade to meet intense competition when that child has no physical or mental affliction, but suffers an almost equal affliction from the fact that in his own home he has never seen a book, he's never heard a bedtime story, or he's never heard perhaps his own parents speak correct English. And he finds himself at the beginning of a ten-year legally required educational experience, almost doomed to a daily proof by the Establishment that he's an inferior person because he cannot compete with children of superior opportunity.

I know also the problem of a child who reaches the third or fourth grade who can't read and write and who must, until he's sixteen, experience each day what must be an absolutely horrible experience of seeing the other children studying mathematics and English and literature and history and civics, when it's all a foreign language to that child.

I also recognize the problem we face with many of our young who have the talent and the ability but don't find the opportunity to pursue their education beyond the high school years, or who quite often lack the proper counseling at home or at school. And the combined deprivation which exists from these needs afflicts us all.

Higher Education Awards Banquet
Atlanta, Georgia
May 9, 1972

The Two Most Regressive Taxes

... THE TWO most regressive taxes, the two which fall heavily on the workingman or the retired people with fixed incomes, are the sales tax and the property tax. Anybody who says he is going to lower your property taxes fifty dollars a year and then raises what you pay in sales tax by a hundred dollars a year with a one-cent increase is not your friend. I am not a party to that sort of con game. I never have been, and I never will be.

Georgia State AFL-CIO Convention
Savannah, Georgia
October 18, 1972

Those Who Are Frozen in Heart and Mind

... THERE ARE conflicts in society: the rich versus the poor, the South versus the North, the black versus the white, the worker versus his employer, the small businessman versus the multinational companies, the liberal versus the conservative. But I think one of the strongest and most persistent conflicts lies between those who are frozen in heart and mind and who have become perpetually old on the one hand, and those who are still young at heart on the other hand.

I am not talking about the number of years that you might have lived, because there are some in this audience today, even though you might only be in your teens, who are already old, who think that you have arrived at a station in life that's adequate because God blessed you.

Your father and mother may be wealthy; you may not ever have been hungry; you may be socially prominent; you may be assured of a college education and a good income for the rest of your life; you may be satisfied with the present or prospective niche that you envision for yourself in society. And you may feel that you don't have to be concerned about those less fortunate than you and those who, because you might occupy a position of leadership in the future, might be dependent on having their own destinies improved by your own actions.

But if you occupy that position and attitude, you are already old. You may be seventeen years old, but you are already old because your mind and your heart have been closed.

Georgia YMCA Youth Assembly
Atlanta, Georgia
April 20, 1973

Conscience and Controversy

... THERE IS a great tendency for all of us to shy away from controversial issues, but I tell you that every issue that is worth anything is bound to be controversial. Too often we avoid taking a stand for what we know to be right because we are afraid we are going to lose a dollar or a client or a vote—and at that moment when we profess our willingness to trade that friend, that dollar, that client, or that vote for a piece of our soul, we lose another chunk out of whatever it is that gives us the right to call ourselves men.

No city, no state, no country can afford men in the professions, in business, or in politics who are more afraid of controversy than of their conscience.

National Conference of Bankruptcy Judges
Atlanta, Georgia
November 1, 1973

Martin Luther King, Jr.

BEFORE I accept this portrait, there are two people that I would like to recognize in a special way. One of them is a young woman who serves on my staff, who has come to me many times to say, "Governor, you have an opportunity to perform a service that will bind all our people together in a common attitude of understanding and communication and love." She has been a constant inspiration to me. Her name is Rita Samuels. She is over in the corner, characteristically not seeking the limelight.

The other person that I would like to recognize again, now that you have seen the product of this great work, is George Mandus, the artist.

As I sat here in the rotunda of our capitol, I looked up at some of the portraits that already hang in there, that I consider to be hallowed halls. To my left, on the next floor, is a portrait of George Washington, our first President. On the right is Thomas Jefferson, a great humanitarian who loved the common people. Here on my left, illuminated, is a portrait of Robert E. Lee, who served in a time of great stress in our nation and who, I think, deserved the devotion and respect of men who knew him personally and the admiration of those of us who have come to know his character.

Now, today, we are unveiling the portrait of another great American....

In the life of Martin Luther King, Jr., our black citizens of Georgia and throughout this nation saw their own aspirations realized, and they saw the prejudices and legal prohibitions against full citizenship begin to be removed. The privileged and powerful leaders of our nation said, "This cannot be."

But I can state to you today a truth that all of you know:

26

that the prediction of Martin Luther King, Jr., that freedom would thus be enhanced among all men has come true.

It would be hard to say who has been more greatly liberated, the black or the white citizens of our nation, because our white citizens have been relieved of a millstone about our necks and of preoccupation with an artificial distinction between the worth of men, which was a handicap to the progress of us all.

I believe we now recognize that we have been liberated, all of us, by granting equality of rights and participation to all Americans regardless of race or color.

Dr. King's works were an inspiration not only to Americans but throughout the earth, and his awarding of the Nobel Peace Prize was recognition of his contributions.

In closing, let me say that as Governor of this state, I am proud of Georgia. I think it is fair to say that I have taken no innovative or courageous action contrary to the inclinations of the five million people I represent. As I said in my inaugural address three years ago, "The time for racial discrimination is over." I said this not to inspire Georgians to change their minds but to recognize, as Secretary of State Ben Fortson well knows, a change that has already taken place in the minds and hearts of the people that I love and represent.

I want my country to be number one. I want the United States of America to be the pre-eminent nation in all the world, but I do not equate pre-eminence solely with military might nor with the ability to subjugate others or to demonstrate prowess on the battlefield. We must have adequate forces to defend ourselves. But, in addition to that, an accomplishment in truth, a recognition of the equality and worth of man, a constant searching for honesty and morality, an openness of government, the ability of all men to control their own destinies and a constant recognition of the values of compassion and love among all our people—these are the proper measures of a great nation.

I accept this portrait of Martin Luther King, Jr., on behalf of all those who live in our state. I believe that it will enhance the education of visiting schoolchildren, both black and white, that it will be an inspiration to all Georgians and to other visitors to our capitol, and that it will stand as a reminder of the proper correlation of natural human frailties in governmental and social affairs with the greatness and purity of our religious principles.

Martin Luther King Portrait
Georgia State Capitol
Atlanta, Georgia
February 17, 1974

A Legitimate Humility

... I RECENTLY shared the podium with Dr. Norman Vincent Peale at a ceremony in Macon, Georgia, when he gave an award on behalf of *Guideposts* magazine to a Macon church. The church has only thirty-five members, all of whom are retarded children; it is the Church of the Exceptional.

I was touched very deeply when during that ceremony a forty-five-year-old retarded child came down the aisle on the arm of a layman, with a torch in her hand. As was her assignment each week, she struggled that evening to light her one candle at the altar. And just as she was almost ready to give up, and the pastor was about to assist her, her candle lit. The whole congregation breathed a sigh of relief, and as she turned around, a beautiful expression on her mongoloid face, she touched the hearts of everyone there. This demonstration of her simple and total commitment had more power than any words any of us had to offer.

I wonder how many of us, lay leaders of the nation, have that completely childlike commitment to Christ that caused a heart to be constantly open, to be constantly self-examined, that fosters a legitimate humility.

Leadership Prayer Breakfast
Orlando, Florida
March 27, 1974

Law Day

Carter's Law Day speech gained unexpected national attention when journalist Hunter Thompson happened to hear it—he was covering Senator Edward Kennedy, who also spoke at Law Day—and wrote a glowing article about it in *Rolling Stone*. Carter's remarks were intended for two more immediate audiences. First, he was letting the leaders of the Georgia bar know that he believed they could do far more than they had done to advance social justice in Georgia. Second, Carter's oldest son, Jack, was in the audience. Jack was in his third year in law school, and Carter feared that law school might narrow his horizons; thus, Carter's Law Day speech was in part an exhortation to his son to see his legal career not simply in terms of self-interest but in terms of public service.

... I'M NOT qualified to talk to you about law, because in addition to being a peanut farmer, I'm an engineer and a nuclear physicist, not a lawyer. I was planning, really, to talk to you more today about politics and the interrelationship of political affairs and law than about what I'm actually going to speak on. But after Senator Kennedy's delightful and very fine response to political questions during his speech, and after his analysis of the Watergate problems, I stopped at a room on the way, while he had his press conference, and I changed my speech notes.

My own interest in the criminal justice system is very deep and heartfelt. Not having studied law, I've had to learn the hard way. I read a lot and listen a lot. One of the sources for my understanding about the proper application of criminal justice and the system of equity is from reading Reinhold Niebuhr, one of his books that Bill Gunter gave me quite a number of years ago. The other source of my understanding about what's right and wrong in this society is from a friend of mine, a poet named Bob Dylan. After listening to his records about "The Lonesome Death of Hattie Caroll" and "Like a Rolling Stone" and "The Times, They Are A-Changin'," I've learned to appreciate the dynamism of change in a modern society.

I grew up as a landowner's son. But I don't think I ever realized the proper interrelationship between the landowner and those who worked on a farm until I heard Dylan's record "I Ain't Gonna Work on Maggie's Farm No More." So I came here speaking to you today about your subject with a base for my information founded on Reinhold Niebuhr and Bob Dylan.

One of the things that Niebuhr says is that the sad duty of the political system is to establish justice in a sinful world. He goes on to say that there's no way to establish or maintain justice without law, that the laws are constantly changing to stabilize the social equilibrium of the forces and counterforces of a dynamic society, and that the law in its totality is an expression of the structure of government.

Well, as a farmer who has now been in office for three years, I've seen firsthand the inadequacy of my own comprehension of what government ought to do for its people. I've had a constant learning process, sometimes from lawyers, sometimes from practical experience, sometimes from failures and mistakes that have been pointed out to me after they were made.

I had lunch this week with the members of the Judicial Selection Committee, and they were talking about a consent search warrant. I said I didn't know what a consent search warrant was. They said, "Well, that's when two policemen go to a house. One of them goes to the front door and knocks on it, and the other one runs around to the back door and yells, 'Come in.'" I have to admit that, as Governor, quite often I search for ways to bring about my own hopes; not quite so stringently testing the law as that, but with a similar motivation.

I would like to talk to you for a few moments about some of the practical aspects of being a governor who is still deeply concerned about the inadequacies of a system of which it is obvious that you're so patently proud.

I have refrained completely from making any judicial appointments on the basis of political support or other factors, and have chosen, in every instance, superior court judges, quite often state judges, appellate court judges, on the basis of merit analysis by a highly competent, open, qualified group of distinguished Georgians. I'm proud of this.

We've now established in the Georgia Constitution a qualifications commission, which for the first time can hear complaints from average citizens about the performance in office of judges and can investigate those complaints and with the status and the force of the Georgia Constitution behind them can remove a judge from office or take corrective steps.

We've now passed a constitutional amendment, which is waiting for the citizenry to approve, that establishes a uniform criminal justice court system in this state so that the affairs of the judiciary can be more orderly structured, so that work loads can be balanced, and so that over a period of time there might be an additional factor of equity, which quite often does not exist now because of the wide disparity among the different courts of Georgia.

We passed this year a judge sentencing bill for non-capital cases with a review procedure. I've had presented to me, by members of the Pardons and Paroles Board, an analysis of some of the sentences given to people by the superior court judges of this state which grieved me deeply and shocked me as a layman. I believe that over a period of time, the fact that a group of other judges can review and comment on the sentences meted out in the different portions of Georgia will bring some more equity to the system.

We have finally eliminated the unsworn statement law in Georgia—the last state to do it.

This year we analyzed in depth the structure of the drug penalties in this state. I believe in the future there will be a clear understanding of the seriousness of different crimes relating to drugs. We've finally been able to get through the Legislature a law that removes alcoholism or drunkenness as a criminal offense. When this law goes into effect next year, I think it will create a new sense of compassion and concern and justice for the roughly 150,000 alcoholics in Georgia, many of whom escape the consequences of what has been a crime because of some social or economic prominence, and will remove a very heavy load from the criminal justice system.

In our prisons, which in the past have been a disgrace to Georgia, we've tried to make substantive changes in the quality of those who administer them and to put a new realm of understanding and hope and compassion into the administration of that portion of the system of justice. Ninety-five percent of those who are presently incarcerated in prisons will be returned to be our neighbors. And now the thrust of the entire program, as initiated under Ellis MacDougall and now continued under Dr. Ault, is to try to discern in the soul of each convicted and sentenced person redeeming features that can be enhanced. We plan a career for that person to be pursued while he is in prison. I believe that the early data that we have on recidivism rates indicates the efficacy of what we've done.

The GBI, which was formerly a matter of great concern to all those who were interested in law enforcement, has now been substantially changed—for the better. I would put it up now in quality against the FBI, the Secret Service, or any other crime control organization in this nation.

Well, does that mean that everything is all right?

It doesn't to me.

I don't know exactly how to say this, but I was thinking just a few moments ago about some of the things that are of deep concern to me as Governor. As a scientist, I was working constantly, along with almost everyone who professes that dedication of life, to probe, probe every day of my life for constant change for the better. It's completely anachronistic in the makeup of a nuclear physicist or an engineer or scientist to be satisfied with what we've got, or to rest on the laurels of past accomplishments. It's the nature of the profession.

As a farmer, the same motivation persists. Every farmer that I know of, who is worth his salt or who's just average, is ahead of the experiment stations and the research agronomist in finding better ways, changing ways to plant, cultivate, utilize herbicides, gather, cure, sell farm products. The competition for innovation is tremendous, equivalent to the realm of nuclear physics even.

In my opinion, it's different in the case of lawyers. And maybe this is a circumstance that is so inherently true that it can't be changed.

I'm a Sunday School teacher, and I've always known that the structure of law is founded on the Christian ethic that you shall love the Lord your God and your neighbor as yourself— a very high and perfect standard. We all know the fallibility of man; and the contentions in society, as described by Reinhold Niebuhr and many others, don't permit us to achieve perfection. We do strive for equality, but not with a fervent and daily commitment. In general, the powerful and the influential in our society shape the laws and have a great influence on the Legislature or the Congress. This creates a reluctance to change, because the powerful and the influential have carved out for themselves or have inherited a privileged position in society, of wealth or social prominence or higher education or opportunity for the future. Quite often those circumstances are circumvented at a very early age because college students, particularly undergraduates, don't have any commitment to the preservation of the way things are. But later, as their interrelationship with the present circumstances grows, they also become committed to approaching change very, very slowly and very, very cautiously, and there's a commitment to the status quo.

I remember when I was a child, I lived on a farm about three miles from Plains, and we didn't have electricity or running water. We lived on the railroad—Seaboard Coast Line Railroad. Like all farm boys I had a flip, a slingshot. They had stabilized the railroad bed with little white round rocks, which I used for ammunition. I would go out frequently to the railroad and gather the most perfectly shaped rocks of proper size. I always had a few in my pockets, and I had others cached away around the farm so that they would be convenient if I ran out of my pocket supply.

One day I was leaving the railroad track with my pockets full of rocks and hands full of rocks, and my mother came out on the front porch—this is not a very interesting story but it illustrates a point—and she had in her hands a plate full of cookies that she had just baked for me. She called me, I am sure with love in her heart, and said, "Jimmy, I've baked some cookies for you." I remember very distinctly walking up to her and standing there for fifteen or twenty seconds, in honest doubt about whether I should drop those rocks which were worthless and take the cookies that my mother had prepared for me, which between her and me were very valuable.

Quite often we have the same inclination in our everyday lives. We don't recognize that change can sometimes be very beneficial, although we fear it. Anyone who lives in the South looks back on the last fifteen to twenty years with some degree of embarrassment, including myself. To think about going back to a county unit system, which deliberately cheated for generations certain white voters of this state, is almost inconceivable. To revert back or to forgo the one man, one vote principle, we would now consider to be a horrible violation of the basic principles of justice and equality and fairness and equity.

The first speech I ever made in the Georgia Senate, representing the most conservative district in Georgia, was concerning the abolition of thirty questions that we had so proudly evolved as a subterfuge to keep black citizens from voting and which we used with a great deal of smirking and pride for decades or generations ever since the War between the States—questions that nobody could answer in this room, but which were applied to every black citizen that came to the Sumter County Courthouse or Webster County Courthouse and said, "I want to vote." I spoke in that chamber, fearful of the news media reporting it back home, but overwhelmed with a commitment to the abolition of that artificial barrier to the rights of an American citizen. I remember the thing that I used in my speech, that a black pencil salesman on the outer door of the Sumter County Courthouse could make a better judgment about who ought to be sheriff than two highly educated professors at Georgia Southwestern College.

Dr. Martin Luther King, Jr., who was perhaps despised by many in this room because he shook up our social structure that benefited us, and demanded simply that black citizens be treated the same as white citizens, wasn't greeted with approbation and accolades by the Georgia Bar Association or the Alabama Bar Association. He was greeted with horror. Still, once that change was made, a very simple but difficult change, no one in his right mind would want to go back to circumstances prior to that juncture in the development of our nation's society.

I don't want to go on and on; I'm part of it. But the point I want to make to you is that we still have a long way to go. In every age or every year, we have a tendency to believe that we've come so far now that there's no way to improve the present system. I'm sure when the Wright Brothers flew at Kitty Hawk, they felt that was the ultimate in transportation. When the first atomic bomb was exploded, that was the ultimate development in nuclear physics, and so forth.

Well, we haven't reached the ultimate. But who's going to search the heart and the soul of an organization like yours or a law school or state or nation and say, "What can we still do to restore equity and justice or to preserve it or to enhance it in this society?"

You know, I'm not afraid to make the change. I don't have anything to lose. But as a farmer I'm not qualified to assess the characteristics of the ninety-one hundred inmates in the Georgia prisons, fifty percent of whom ought not to be there —they ought to be on probation or under some other supervision—and assess what the results of previous court rulings might bring to bear on their lives.

I was in the Governor's Mansion for two years, enjoying the services of a very fine cook, who was a prisoner—a woman. One day she came to me, after she got over her two years of timidity, and said, "Governor, I would like to borrow two hundred and fifty dollars from you."

I said, "I'm not sure that a lawyer would be worth that much."

She said, "I don't want to hire a lawyer, I want to pay the judge."

I thought it was a ridiculous statement for her; I felt that she was ignorant. But I found out she wasn't. She had been sentenced by a superior court judge in the state, who still serves, to seven years or seven hundred and fifty dollars. She had raised, early in her prison career, five hundred dollars. I didn't lend her the money, but I had Bill Harper, my legal aide, look into it. He found the circumstances were true. She was quickly released under a recent court ruling that had come down in the last few years.

I was down on the coast this weekend. I was approached by a woman who asked me to come by her home. I went by, and she showed me documents that indicated that her illiterate mother, who had a son in jail, had gone to the county surveyor in that region and had borrowed two hundred and twenty-five dollars to get her son out of jail. She had a letter from the justice of the peace that showed that her mother had made a mark on a blank sheet of paper. They paid off the two hundred and twenty-five dollars, and she has the receipts to show it. Then they started a five-year program trying to get back the paper she signed, without success. They went to court. The lawyer that had originally advised her to sign the paper showed up as the attorney for the surveyor. She had put up fifty acres of land near the county seat as security. When she got to court, she found that instead of signing a security deed, that she had signed a warranty deed. That case has already been appealed to the Supreme Court, and she lost.

Well, I know that the technicalities of the law that would permit that are probably justifiable. She didn't have a good lawyer. My heart feels and cries out that something ought to be analyzed, not just about the structure of government, judicial qualification councils, and judicial appointment committees, and eliminating the unsworn statement. Those things are important. But they don't reach the crux of the point—that now we assign punishment to fit the criminal and not the crime.

You can go in the prisons of Georgia, and I don't know, it may be that poor people are the only ones who commit crimes, but I do know they are the only ones who serve prison sentences. When Ellis MacDougall first went to Reidsville, he found people that had been in solitary confinement for ten years. We now have five hundred misdemeanants in the Georgia prison system.

Well, I don't know the theory of law, but there is one other point I want to make, just for your own consideration. I think we've made great progress in the Pardons and Paroles Board since I've been in office and since we've reorganized the government. We have five very enlightened people there now. And on occasion they go out to the prison system to interview the inmates, to decide whether or not they are worthy to be released after they serve one-third of their sentence. I think most jurors and most judges feel that when they give the sentence they know that after a third of the sentence has gone by they will be eligible for careful consideration. Just think a moment about your own son or your own father or your own daughter being in prison, having served seven years of a lifetime term and being considered for a release. Don't you think that they ought to be examined and the Pardons and Paroles Board ought to look them in the eye and ask them a question and, if they are turned down, ought to give them some substantive reason why they are not released and what they can do to correct their defect?

I do.

I think it's just as important at their time for consideration of early release as it is even when they are sentenced. But I don't know how to bring about that change.

We had an ethics bill in the State Legislature this year. Half of it passed—to require an accounting for contributions during a campaign—but the part that applied to people after the campaign failed. We couldn't get through a requirement for revelation of payments or gifts to officeholders after they are in office.

The largest force against that ethics bill was the lawyers.

Some of you here tried to help get a consumer protection package passed without success.

The regulatory agencies in Washington are made up not of people to regulate industries but of representatives of the industries that are regulated. Is that fair and right and equitable? I don't think so.

I'm only going to serve four years as Governor, as you know. I think that's enough. I enjoy it, but I think I've done all I can in the Governor's office. I see the lobbyists in the State Capitol, filling the halls on occasions. Good people, competent people, the most pleasant, personable, extroverted citizens of Georgia. Those are the characteristics that are required for a lobbyist. They represent good folks. But I tell you that when a lobbyist goes to represent the Peanut Warehousemen's Association of the Southeast, which I belong to, which I helped to organize, they go there to represent the peanut warehouseman. They don't go there to represent the customers of the peanut warehouseman.

When the State Chamber of Commerce lobbyists go there, they go there to represent the businessman of Georgia. They don't go there to represent the customers of the businessman of Georgia.

When your own organization is interested in some legislation there in the Capitol, they're interested in the welfare or prerogatives or authority of the lawyers. They are not there to represent in any sort of exclusive way the client of the lawyers.

The American Medical Association and its Georgia equivalent—they represent the doctors, who are fine people. But they certainly don't represent the patients of a doctor.

As an elected governor, I feel that responsibility; but I also know that my qualifications are slight—compared to the doctors or the lawyers or the teachers—to determine what's best for the client or the patient or the schoolchild.

This bothers me; and I know that if there was a commitment on the part of the cumulative group of attorneys in this state to search with a degree of commitment and fervency, to eliminate many of the inequities that I've just described that I thought of this morning, our state could be transformed in the attitude of its people toward the government.

Senator Kennedy described the malaise that exists in this nation, and it does.

In closing, I'd like to just illustrate the point by something that came to mind this morning when I was talking to Senator Kennedy about his trip to Russia.

When I was about twelve years old, I liked to read, and I had a school principal named Miss Julia Coleman. Judge Marshall knows her. She forced me pretty much to read, read, read, classical books. She would give me a gold star when I read ten and a silver star when I read five.

One day she called me in and said, "Jimmy, I think it's time for you to read *War and Peace*." I was completely relieved, because I thought it was a book about cowboys and Indians.

Well, I went to the library and checked it out, and it was 1450 pages thick, I think, written by Tolstoy, as you know, about Napoleon's entry into Russia in the 1812–1815 era. He had never been defeated and he was sure he could win, but he underestimated the severity of the Russian winter and the peasants' love for their land.

To make a long story short, the next spring he retreated in defeat. The course of history was changed; it probably affected our own lives.

The point of the book is, and what Tolstoy points out in the epilogue is, that he didn't write the book about Napoleon or the Czar of Russia or even the generals, except on rare occasion. He wrote it about the students and the housewives and the barbers and the farmers and the privates in the army. And the point of the book is that the course of human events, even the greatest historical events, are not determined by the leaders of a nation or a state, like presidents or governors or senators. They are controlled by the combined wisdom and courage and commitment and discernment and unselfishness and compassion and love and idealism of the common ordinary people. If that was true in the case of Russia, where they had a czar, or France, where they had an emperor, how much more true is it in our own case where the Constitution charges us with a direct responsibility for determining what our government is and ought to be?

Well, I've read parts of the embarrassing transcripts, and

I've seen the proud statement of a former Attorney General who protected his boss and now brags on the fact that he tiptoed through a minefield and came out "clean." I can't imagine somebody like Thomas Jefferson tiptoeing through a minefield on the technicalities of the law, and then bragging about being clean afterwards.

I think our people demand more than that. I believe that everyone in this room who is in a position of responsibility as a preserver of the law in its purest form ought to remember the oath that Thomas Jefferson and others took when they practically signed their own death warrant writing the Declaration of Independence—to preserve justice and equity and freedom and fairness, they pledged their lives, their fortunes, and their sacred honor.

University of Georgia
Athens, Georgia
May 4, 1974

Why Not the Best?

WE AMERICANS are a great and diverse people. We take full advantage of our right to develop wide-ranging interests and responsibilities. For instance, I am a farmer, an engineer, a businessman, a planner, a scientist, a governor, and a Christian. Each of you is an individual and different from all the others.

Yet we Americans have shared one thing in common: a belief in the greatness of our country.

We have dared to dream great dreams for our nation. We have taken quite literally the promises of decency, equality, and freedom, of an honest and responsible government.

What has now become of these great dreams?

- That all Americans stand equal before the law;
- That we enjoy a right to pursue health, happiness, and prosperity in privacy and safety;
- That government be controlled by its citizens and not the other way around;
- That this country set a standard within the community of nations of courage, compassion, integrity, and dedication to basic human rights and freedoms.

Our commitment to these dreams has been sapped by debilitating compromise, acceptance of mediocrity, subservience to special interests, and an absence of executive vision and direction.

Having worked during the last twenty years in local, state, and national affairs, I have learned a great deal about our people.

I tell you that their great dreams still live within the collective heart of this nation.

Recently we have discovered that our trust has been betrayed. The veils of secrecy have seemed to thicken around Washington. The purposes and goals of our country are uncertain and sometimes even suspect.

Our people are understandably concerned about this lack of competence and integrity. The root of the problem is not so much that our people have lost confidence in government but that government has demonstrated time and again its lack of confidence in the people.

In our homes or at worship we are ever reminded of what we ought to do and what we ought to be. Our government can and must represent the best and the highest ideals of those of us who voluntarily submit to its authority.

Politicians who seek to further their political careers through appeals to our doubts, fears, and prejudices will be exposed and rejected.

For too long political leaders have been isolated from the people. They have made decisions from an ivory tower. Few have ever seen personally the direct impact of government programs involving welfare, prisons, mental institutions, unemployment, school busing, or public housing. Our people feel that they have little access to the core of government and little influence with elected officials.

Now it is time for this chasm between people and government to be bridged and for American citizens to join in shaping our nation's future.

Now is the time for new leadership and new ideas to make a reality of these dreams, still held by our people.

To begin with, the confidence of people in our own government must be restored.

Specific steps must be taken.

- We need an all-inclusive sunshine law in Washington so that special interests will not retain their exclusive access behind closed doors.
- Absolutely no gifts of value should ever again be permitted to a public official.

- Complete revelation of all business and financial involvements of major officials should be required, and none should be continued which constitute a possible conflict with the public interest.
- Regulatory agencies must not be managed by representatives of the industry being regulated, and no personnel transfers between agency and the industry should be made within a period of four full years.
- Public financing of campaigns should be extended to members of Congress.
- The activities of lobbyists must be more thoroughly revealed and controlled.
- Minimum secrecy within government should be matched with maximum personal privacy for private citizens.
- All federal judges, diplomats, and other major officials should be selected on a strict basis of merit.
- For many years in the State Department we have chosen from among almost sixteen thousand applicants about a hundred and ten of our nation's finest young leaders to represent us in the international world. But we top this off with the disgraceful and counterproductive policy of appointing unqualified persons to major diplomatic posts as political payoffs. This must be stopped immediately.
- Every effort should be extended to encourage full participation by our people in their own government's processes, including universal voter registration for elections.
- We must insure better public understanding of executive policy, and better exchange of ideas between the Congress and the White House. To do this, Cabinet members representing the President should meet in scheduled public-interrogation sessions with the full bodies of Congress.

- All our citizens must know that they will be treated fairly.
- To quote from my own inauguration speech of four years ago: "The time for racial discrimination is over. Our people have already made this major and difficult decision, but we cannot underestimate the challenge of hundreds of minor decisions yet to be made. . . . No poor, rural, weak, or black person should ever have to bear the additional burden of being deprived of the opportunity for an education, a job, or simple justice."
- We must meet this firm national commitment without equivocation or timidity in every aspect of private and public life.

As important as honesty and openness are, they are not enough. There must also be substance and logical direction in government.

The mechanism of our government should be understandable, efficient, and economical . . . and it can be.

We must give top priority to a drastic and thorough revision of the federal bureaucracy, to its budgeting system, and to the procedures for analyzing the effectiveness of its many varied services. Tight businesslike management and planning techniques must be instituted and maintained, utilizing the full authority and personal involvement of the President himself.

This is no job for the fainthearted. It will be met with violent opposition from those who now enjoy a special privilege, those who prefer to work in the dark, or those whose private freedoms are threatened.

A government that is honest and competent, with clear purpose and strong leadership, can work with the American people to meet the challenges of the present and the future.

We can then face together the tough long-range solutions to our economic woes. Our people are ready to make personal sacrifices when clear national economic policies are devised and understood.

We are grossly wasting our energy resources and other precious raw materials as though their supply were infinite. We must even face the prospect of changing our basic ways of living. This change will either be made on our own initiative in a planned and rational way, or forced on us with chaos and suffering by the inexorable laws of nature.

Energy imports and consumption must be reduced, free competition enhanced by rigid enforcement of antitrust laws, and general monetary growth restrained. Pinpointed federal programs can ease the more acute pains of recession, such as now exist in the construction industry. We should consider extension of unemployment compensation, the stimulation of investments, public subsidizing of employment, and surtaxes on excess profits.

We are still floundering and equivocating about protection of our environment. Neither designers of automobiles, mayors of cities, power companies, farmers, nor those of us who simply have to breathe the air, love beauty, and would like to fish or swim in pure water have the slightest idea in God's world what is coming out of Washington next! What does come next must be a firm commitment to pure air, clean water, and unspoiled land.

Almost twenty years after its conception we have not finished the basic interstate highway system. To many lobbyists who haunt the capitol buildings of the nation, ground transportation still means only more highways and more automobiles—the bigger the better. We must have a national commitment to transportation capabilities which will encourage the most efficient movement of American people and cargo.

Gross tax inequities are being perpetuated. The surely taxed income is that which is derived from the sweat of manual labor. Carefully contrived loopholes let the total tax burden shift more and more toward the average wage earner.

The largest corporations pay the lowest tax rates, and some with very high profits pay no tax at all.

Every American has a right to expect that laws will be administered in an evenhanded manner, but it seems that something is wrong even with our system of justice. Defendants who are repeatedly out on bail commit more crimes. Aggravating trial delays and endless litigation are common.

Citizens without influence often bear the brunt of prosecution while violators of antitrust laws and other white-collar criminals are ignored and go unpunished.

Following recent presidential elections, our U.S. Attorney General has replaced the Postmaster General as the chief political appointee; and we have recently witnessed the prostitution of this most important law enforcement office. Special prosecutors had to be appointed simply to insure enforcement of the law! The Attorney General should be removed from politics.

Is a simplified, fair, and compassionate welfare program beyond the capacity of our American government? I think not.

The quality of health care in this nation depends largely on economic status. It is often unavailable or costs too much.

Is a practical and comprehensive national health program beyond the capacity of our American government? I think not.

As a farmer, I have been appalled at the maladministration of our nation's agricultural economy. We have seen the elimination of our valuable food reserves, which has contributed to wild fluctuations in commodity prices and wiped out dependable trade and export capabilities. Grain speculators and monopolistic processors have profited, while farmers are going bankrupt trying to produce food that consumers are going broke trying to buy.

I know this nation can develop an agricultural policy that will insure a fair profit to our farmers and a fair price to consumers.

Our nation's security is obviously of paramount importance, and everything must be done to insure adequate military preparedness. But there is no reason why our national
defense establishment cannot also be efficient.

Misdirected efforts such as the construction of unnecessary
pork-barrel projects by the Corps of Engineers must be
terminated.

The biggest waste and danger of all is the unnecessary
proliferation of atomic weapons throughout the world. Our
ultimate goal should be the elimination of nuclear weapon
capability among all nations. In the meantime, simple, careful, and firm proposals to implement this mutual arms reduction should be pursued as a prime national purpose in all our
negotiations with nuclear powers—present or potential.

Is the achievement of these and other goals beyond the
capacity of our American government? I think not.

About three months ago I met with the governors of the
other twelve original states in Philadelphia. Exactly two hundred years after the convening of the First Continental Congress we walked down the same streets, then turned left and
entered a small building named Carpenter's Hall. There we
heard exactly the same prayer and sat in the same chairs
occupied in September of 1774 by Samuel Adams, John Jay,
John Adams, Patrick Henry, George Washington, and about
forty-five other strong and opinionated leaders.

They held widely divergent views and they debated for
weeks. They and others who joined them for the Second
Continental Congress avoided the production of timid compromise resolutions. They were somehow inspired, and they
reached for greatness. Their written premises formed the
basis on which our nation was begun.

I don't know whose chair I occupied, but sitting there, I
thought soberly about their times and ours. Their people
were also discouraged, disillusioned, and confused. But these
early leaders acted with purpose and conviction.

I wondered to myself: Were they more competent, more

intelligent, or better educated than we? Were they more courageous? Did they have more compassion or love for their neighbors? Did they have deeper religious convictions? Were they more concerned about the future of their children than we?

I think not.

We are equally capable of correcting our faults, overcoming difficulties, managing our own affairs, and facing the future with justifiable confidence.

I am convinced that among us two hundred million Americans there is a willingness—even eagerness—to restore in our country what has been lost—if we have understandable purposes and goals and a modicum of bold and inspired leadership.

Our government can express the highest common ideals of human beings—if we demand of it standards of excellence.

It is now time to stop and to ask ourselves the question which my last commanding officer, Admiral Hyman Rickover, asked me and every other young naval officer who serves or has served in an atomic submarine.

For our nation—for all of us—that question is "Why not the best?"

Announcement Speech, National Press Club
Washington, D.C.
December 12, 1974

2

Toward
the
Nomination

1975–1976

Two Very Basic Concerns

LET ME tell you a little about myself and about my campaign, and I'll answer your questions.

I consider the Presidency of this country, as you probably do, the most important political office in the world. I think it deserves my own full-time commitment, and I am a full-time candidate. I have scheduled for this year outside the State of Georgia two hundred and fifty days to work on the campaign itself, which gives me about a day and a half a week to my own state. I intend to enter all the primaries, which is a major undertaking and one that I have considered very carefully. That includes the primaries in the State of Texas, the State of Alabama, and others.

I am a farmer. I grow certified seed on my farm. I have a very prosperous business, one I can afford to leave for the next nine and half years—for the campaign and two terms in the White House. It's one I started myself. I came home from the Navy, and I lived in a government housing project, and I was my only employee for three years, except my wife...

I am a businessman. I am almost a professional planner. I was the first state president of the Georgia Planning Association.

I'm an engineer, and my graduate work is in nuclear physics. I've been in the Georgia Senate for four years and the Governor's office for four years, and before that I was chairman of a county school board for seven years. So I have a pretty good background in local, state, and federal government.

I decided to run for President two and a half years ago, shortly after the Democratic convention, and I have been working on it in a very careful and meticulous way ever since. I look forward to the campaign, and I approach it with a great deal of anticipation and confidence. I don't intend to lose. There are a lot of challenges and that suits me just fine. My own style of campaigning in a presidential election will be similar to what I used in Georgia. My opponent was a very handsome, rich, young, popular ex-governor named Carl Sanders. He had the endorsement of all the newspapers in Atlanta except one. Almost all the lawyers endorsed him, almost all the legislators. But I carried a hundred and fifty counties; he carried nine. Some of those counties I carried with ninety-one percent. I did it by going directly to the voters themselves and presenting myself to them.

In my travels around the country I have found two very basic concerns which I share with the American people. Perhaps you feel them too. One is that our government in Washington has lost its basic integrity. There is no representation in our federal government now of what the American people either are or would like to be, and I don't think this is an inherent characteristic of our nation or its government.

The other concern is that government in Washington is incompetent to deal with the very complicated and growing problems and opportunities of our people. Again, I don't think the government is inherently incompetent.

When I was elected as Governor of Georgia, I went to the office not as a politician, although I don't apologize for that word, but I went there as a planner, as a businessman, as a scientist; and we made some profound changes in the government, which I intend to make in Washington if I am elected. We had three hundred departments and agencies in the Georgia government. We abolished 278 of them, and we established a very fine, simple organization structure with what was left that works. It is open to the Georgia people for their comprehension and control.

We passed a sunshine law that opened up the deliberations of all our state executive and legislative meetings to the news media, even including conference committees between the House and Senate this year. We have put in effect a new budgeting technique for the first time in the world that I devised during my previous campaign called zero-base budgeting. We have had it now for four years, and it works. It is the finest analytic tool that I know of. We strip down the Georgia government each year to zero, and we carefully assess every single delivery system in the state government.

We have specific goals written for every aspect of Georgia's government—in mental health, physical health, alcoholism, drug control, education, transportation, prison reform, and others. We have set down in writing what we hope to do at the end of two years or five years or, in some instances, twenty to twenty-five years. So the Georgia people can constantly be debating about the future of our state; and if they agree on what we hope to achieve, we can work with a common purpose and in concert with one another. None of these things, as you well know, has been done in Washington. In my opinion, all of them can be done; and if I am elected President, all of them will be done. I think the government can be competent. I think the government can be as honest, as unselfish, as decent, as open, as are the American people.

I'm laying my groundwork for the primary campaigns this year, and I'll continue my present rate of campaigning throughout 1975, and then in 1976 I intend to pick up the pace a little bit. I feel prepared for it. I've got a fine group of advisers. I expect to set out very clearly what are my stands on the issues.

I like the ordeal of repeated primary contests because I want my own character to be revealed to the American people—my strengths, my weaknesses, my stand on the issues, no matter how controversial they might be. I want the American people to know what I am. And if I can measure up to what the American people would like for their government to be, as exemplified by the President, then I'll win. If I can't measure up to those expectations—and I hope the standards are very high—then I don't deserve to be President.

I don't have to be President. There are a lot of things I would not do to be elected. I wouldn't tell a lie. I wouldn't make a misleading statement. I wouldn't betray a trust. I wouldn't avoid a controversial issue. If I do any of those things, don't support me, because I wouldn't deserve to lead this country.

I think with Watergate, economic setbacks, and confusion in Washington that maybe the two hundredth birthday of our country, the 1976 election, will be quite different from the ones in the past. As you all well know, the new Democratic Party rules change the strategy involved in campaigning profoundly; and I think the change is basically a help to me. I'll be there when the last vote is counted. I'm not going to withdraw. I'm not interested in being Vice President. I'm not interested in being in a Cabinet. I'm not interested in going to the convention with a strategy based on its being deadlocked, as some of the other candidates are doing. I'm going to the convention with as many delegates as I can win openly and in solid combat, and any negotiations done for me or by me will be in the open. I won't consider my delegates pawns to be shuffled around or traded. If I can't win the Presidency openly without secrecy, then I can't expect to be President openly and without secrecy.

So I look forward to the future with a great deal of anticipation and confidence. I enjoy it. I'm learning a lot about this country, what it is and what it ought to be; and I think the testing in the primaries is very helpful to me, and I think the debate on the issues will be very helpful to the country. I feel, as I say, confident; and I'd like to have your support. But right now I'd like to have your questions.

Luncheon Speech
Baltimore, Maryland
April 2, 1975

News Conference

Q. Why do you think the climate is such that a Southern governor can be elected now?

A. Well, the main handicap that a Southern constituency has always had in the past has been our preoccupation with the race issue. And we, I think, have successfully solved that problem and have removed in effect that millstone of racial preoccupation from around our necks. I might say that every civil rights leader in the nation who has expressed a preference so far has already endorsed me for President; and as I have traveled around more than half the states since late January, I honestly have not detected any prejudice against me because I am a Southerner.

I think the Southern people are proud enough and advanced enough politically now so that we are no longer satisfied with just sending a message to Washington as we have tried to do in the past with Strom Thurmond and George Wallace and others. I think that it's time for the Presidency to actually be originated in the South and for the South to send a President to Washington. I happened to have lived all over the country, and I am familiar with the rest of the nation and I feel completely confident that the prejudice that is ordinarily ascribed to other Americans about the South has been exaggerated. I don't think the prejudice is there anymore.

Q. Governor Bumpers, just the other day while he was home, described all those currently running for President as on ego trips. Are you on an ego trip?

A. Well, I hate to disagree with my good friend Dale, but I am sure that when he said that he was not talking about me. I think that anybody who aspires to higher office such as

the Presidency would have to have a high opinion of themselves. I think probably politicians are about half ego and
about half humility. I think I have my share of both of them.
Q. What if Senator Bumpers decides to run?
A. If Senator Bumpers decides to run, he is going to have
to whip me, and I don't think he can.
Q. Are you the liberal answer to George Wallace?
A. I don't think so. I've always been liberal on the race issue,
on environmental questions, and on human justice, but I consider myself to be a tough conservative on the management
of government. As a farmer and as a businessman, as an engineer, I have tried to bring those attributes to the management of Georgia's government, and I think that any businessman in the state would tell you that my administration
has taken a competent and conservative approach to the
management of the government and the management of the
taxpayers' money. I would bring the same approach to Washington, but I think it would be hard to ascribe any particular
label to me or to any other person.
Q. Do you think Ford will be the nominee of the Republicans?
A. Yes, I do think that. I am convinced that if President Ford
wants to be the nominee, he will, and my presumption now
is that he will want to be the nominee.
Q. What do you see as the issues?
A. Well, the issues exist in the minds of the people. I don't
think a candidate can contrive issues and say that this is the
kind of issue I want to run on.
Q. Do you think that if he runs, the issue will be primarily
an economic one?
A. I think economic, and if President Ford runs, I think it
would be an assessment of whether or not he is a leader. I
think that President Ford is a good, honest, decent person.
I know him well and have known him long before he became
President. His wife has visited in our home. I have been with

him often. I think he is a very weak leader. I don't think that he shows any boldness or aggressiveness. I think he is a typical product of a lifetime in the Congress, where everything is handled incrementally and through compromise.

Q. Who do you think will be the leading candidates? Excluding yourself, who else? Jackson tried to be . . .

A. I personally think that Jackson has already peaked, but that may be an underestimation of his strength.

Q. How about Bentsen?

A. Bentsen is probably in the race to stay. Udall in my judgment is still trying to decide whether or not to run. I think that, to be perfectly frank, Fred Harris and Gene McCarthy are just kind of fringe candidates. Wallace—I don't know if he will run or not. I presume that he will. But if those that I just named stayed in the race, I don't know who else might run, I would guess possibly that Birch Bayh would consider it if a vacuum does not exist. And Frank Church has been mentioned from Idaho—a very fine senator, he's involved in one of the many CIA investigations. I think he will probably finish that up before he gets involved, but they will be getting started eight or ten months after I have already started working.

Little Rock, Arkansas
April 11, 1975

I Intend to Win

THE MAIN thing I want to do this afternoon in about an hour is to get to know how you feel about our country and to let you know about myself, because I'm completely convinced that I'm going to be the next President of this country.

In the last two years, almost three, I've been in eleven foreign nations. I've been in forty-seven states, all but Montana and the two Dakotas.

I've talked a lot and I've listened a lot. I don't think any human being in the whole country has traveled more or met with more diverse groups or listened to more questions or answered more questions than have I.

And there are two basic questions that I hear everywhere. No matter whether someone is out of work or rich, farmer or city dweller, black or white, rural or urban—it doesn't matter. There are two basic questions that we're going to have to face.

The first one is: Can our system of government, as we know it, continue to exist? Can the mechanism of our federal government, the bureaucracy, possibly be well organized? Can it be efficient, economical, purposeful? Can the President once again work in harmony with the Congress to meet the needs of our nation? Is it possible for the federal, state, and local levels of government to share, in a predictable way, responsibilities for exactly the same constituents? Can our government be competent?

A vast majority of the people in this country think the answer is no. I think the answer is yes.

The other question is this—a little more personal but perhaps even more important—Can our government in Washington, which we love, be decent? Is it possible for it to be honest and truthful and fair and idealistic, compassionate, filled with love? Is it possible for our government to be what the American people are, or what we would like to be? Can it once again be a source of pride instead of apology and shame and embarrassment?

A lot of people think the answer is no. I think the answer is yes.

We still have a system of government that's the best on earth. The vision that was ours two hundred years ago is still there. Our Constitution still says the same thing. Equality, equity, fairness, decency, are still aspects of our government. Freedom, liberty, individualism, are still integral aspects of our government. We've got a nation of which we ought to be proud. But, I tell you, there are a lot of things about this country that are no longer a source of pride. Our tax structure is a disgrace to the human race. The surest income to be taxed is the income earned from manual labor. There is no secret loophole for someone who draws a paycheck every week or every two weeks. The average family in this country that makes less than $10,000 a year pays a higher proportion of its income in taxes than the average family that makes more than $1 million a year.

We need to break up the sweetheart arrangement that exists between regulatory agencies and industries being regulated. It's kind of a revolving door. The people go out into the industries that are being regulated, they come back into the government regulatory agencies. There's no way to tell where the federal energy agencies stop and the major oil companies start. They're the same people—the same technicians, the same administrators. Our federal energy policy is overly simplistic. It's not designed for the consumers, it's designed by and for the major oil companies, and President Ford is their spokesman. It's "raise the price of oil as much as possible as quickly as possible." Period.

I'm a military man. I graduated from Annapolis. I served eleven years in the Navy, most of the time in submarines. I was a senior officer of the crew that built the second atomic submarine—the *Sea Wolf*. I know the Defense Department fairly well. And I can tell you again, accurately, that the most wasteful bureaucracy in Washington is in the Pentagon. And it ought not to be that way. We need a tough, simple well-organized, muscular defense capability. But we don't need a horrible, bloated bureaucracy.

We've also got too much dependence in this country on atomic weapons.

When I make my Inaugural Address, early in 1977, I'm going to spell out that the purpose of this country is to reduce atomic weapons in all nations to zero. Because we've got a need to let the rest of the world know where we stand. It may not happen completely in my lifetime, but every time we negotiate with a nuclear power we ought to constantly press them, "Let's cut back in atomic weapons."

The last thing I want to say is this, and then I'll answer your questions. I'm from the South; maybe most of you are too. And we've come a long way in the South. It used to be that we had a millstone around our neck, or an albatross, of racism. And it's no credit to me or to you or to your parents that for generations we sat mute and scared while black people were deprived of a right to vote or a right to get a job or to live where they wanted to or to get an education or to have simple justice.

We've come a long way; we've got a long way to go in this country. We ought to constantly be searching for a way to make our nation more decent and more fair. We've accepted lower standards for our country than we would for ourselves.

Our country is strong in international affairs. And we ought to once again assert our leadership, because we've lost it. But that leadership ought not to be based on military might or political pressure or economic power, but on the basis of fact that this country in its foreign affairs is honest and truthful and fair and predictable.

I don't see any difference in the morality that we ought to assert in foreign affairs than what the character of the American people is. We've fallen so far short in so many different ways that we ought to correct it.

I don't intend to lose the election. I'm not going to withdraw. I'm not interested in being Vice President. I'll be there when the last vote's counted in Madison Square Garden in July.

I've come here to ask you for your support. The Florida primary is going to be crucial, perhaps the most important in the whole nation. It takes place the ninth of March. This is George Wallace's strongest state. I don't know if you're proud of that or not. But in 1972 Wallace carried all sixty-seven counties in Florida. I'm determined that Wallace will do much worse in '76 than he did in '72.

I intend to win. Being elected President is very important to me. But it is not the most important thing in my life. I don't have to be President. There are a lot of things that I would not do to be elected. I would never tell a lie. I would never make a misleading statement. I would never betray your trust in me. And I will never avoid a controversial issue.

I'd like for you to watch me very closely. Because I won't be any better President than I am a candidate. If I should ever do any of those things, don't support me. Because I would not be worthy to be President of this country. But I don't intend to do any of them, because my faith and my confidence and my support and my criticism and my advice come from people like you, who don't want anything selfish out of government, who just want us to have once again a nation with a government that is as honest and decent and fair and competent and truthful and idealistic as are the

American people. If we could just have a government once again as good as our people are, that'll be a great achievement.

And I believe that 1976 is the time to do it. And to prove to the rest of the world—and more importantly to the folks in this country of ours—that we still live in the greatest nation on earth.

Florida State University
Tallahassee, Florida
September 28, 1975

It's the Poor Who Suffer

WE'VE COME a long way, as I say, in the South, and in the rest of the nation. I've seen a time in Georgia, not much more than a year ago, when I and Andrew Young and Dr. King and Coretta King and Reverend Abernathy and Julian Bond and others sat in the State Capitol in Georgia and unveiled a painting of Dr. Martin Luther King, Jr., to honor him as one of the great Georgians, and the Ku Klux Klan was marching around the Capitol in protest, and we joined hands with the Secretary of State of Georgia, a gentleman in a wheelchair named Ben Fortson, and we sang together "We Shall Overcome." That could not have been done in the State of Georgia fifteen years ago or ten years ago or five years ago. But it was well received by the black and the white people of our state, because we recognized that what Dr. King did and what Andrew Young did, and many of you perhaps or your parents, liberated not just black people but it liberated white people too, who for generations had a stigma, a millstone, an albatross around our neck, of preoccupation with the race issue.

We need to see black people incorporated into the decision-making processes of our nation. We've been slowly changing the South. I am ashamed to say that I was the first governor who ever appointed a black person to be a judge. Senator Horace Ward was the first one that I appointed. He had been the student who tried to integrate the Georgia Law School years ago, and he won his case; but he won after he had finished law school somewhere else. Now he is a judge. State Representative Julian Bond ran for the Senate and took Horace Ward's place. I am ashamed to say that I was the first governor who ever appointed black people to be on our Board of Regents, Board of Education, Human Resources, barbers' boards, beauticians' boards, to determine who could be a licensed practical nurse or registered nurse.

Those times have changed, but they haven't changed at the federal government level. Can you imagine a black attorney being appointed a federal district court judge in the Southeast? If I am elected President, and I intend to be, there will be black lawyers appointed to those positions, because quite often governors and presidents come and go, but those basic policy-making places have to be filled by those who are knowledgeable and understand the needs not just of poor people but those who are poor and also have suffered discrimination in other ways because of their race or status in life.

QUESTION: What do you think is the most pressing problem in black America today?

CARTER: I can't point out to you any more clearly than you would know yourselves the special problems of black people, but I tell you that in almost every characteristic of government, in criminal justice, for example, it's the poor who suffer.

I have been in every single prison in Georgia to visit while I was Governor and there's one characteristic of the inmates there: they're poor. They're poor. And quite often they are not well educated. The average education level is only five years of schooling. Thirty-five percent of the inmates in Georgia prisons, and I would guess Florida's prisons, are mentally retarded. That's not right or fair.

That is just one indication of the needs that we have.

Where are the streets paved last in your county? You know where they were paved last.

Where are the poorest educational facilities in your county? You know.

What farms are the last ones visited by the county agents in your county? Who are the people who have the last access to a doctor or registered nurse? You know.

Where is the last place served effectively by the rapid transit system or the bus system in a community? You know. Among black people.

Well, all those things need to be changed, and they can only be changed by someone who cares and who is willing to share the responsibility with knowledgeable, effective, dynamic, aggressive spokemen, both black and white. But the best way I know to make sure licensed practical nurse examinations don't discriminate against black applicants is to have black LPN's on the examining board. And the same with beauty parlor operators and barbers and doctors and dentists and funeral directors. That's where the changes need to be made, there and at the top. You can name almost any sort of thing that affects poor people and it affects poor black people much worse.

Being elected President is very important to me. I am going to do all I can to win, and I hope you will join me in it and let me have your advice and your political support and also your tough criticisms and advice.

It is important to be elected, but it's not the most important thing in my life. I don't have to be elected President. There are a lot of things I would not do to be elected. I would like for you to listen closely, because I mean it.

I will never tell a lie. I will never make a misleading statement. I will never betray the confidence that any of you has in me. And I will never avoid a controversial issue.

I won't be any better President than I am a candidate. Watch the television, listen to the radio; if you ever see me do any of those things, don't support me. Because I would not be worthy to be the President of this country.

But I don't intend to do any of those things, because my faith and my confidence and my support and my criticism and my advice comes from people like you. Who don't want anything selfish out of government, but just want to be treated fairly. You want to see us once again have a nation that is as good and honest, decent, truthful, and competent and compassionate and as filled with love as are the American people.

Bethune-Cookman College
Daytona Beach, Florida
October 29, 1975

An Inevitable Role of Leadership

I'M VERY pleased to be here to participate in a discussion that's of great importance to our people. Ordinarily during a presidential campaign, unless our nation is actually at war, we have an inadequate amount of attention paid to foreign affairs....

In looking back, almost every time we've made a serious mistake as we relate to other nations—and we've made a lot of them—it's been because the American people have basically been excluded from participation in the evolution or consummation of attitudes toward other countries around the world. In Vietnam, Chile, Cambodia, Pakistan, the CIA revelations, there's been very little actual involvement of the American people as the decisions were made. We've been excluded, we've been lied to, and we have lost the tremendous advantage of the idealism and the common sense and the basic honesty and character of American people which should accurately exemplify and be exemplified by our nation's own character as it relates to other countries.

I hope we've learned some lessons. One lesson is that we should cease trying to intervene militarily in the internal affairs of other countries unless our own nation is endangered. If it were possible for us to establish democracy all over the world by military force, you might arouse an argument for it. But the attempt to do that is counterproductive. We've seen that vividly in South Korea and also in South Vietnam.

The Soviet Union, with the exception of street skirmishes in Hungary and Czechoslovakia, hasn't lost a single soldier in combat since the Second World War. We lost thirty-four thousand in South Korea and fifty thousand in South Vietnam, basically trying to tell other people what kind of government they ought to have, what kind of leader they should have—and it doesn't work. Either you have a repressive government taking away liberty from their people, as is the case in South Korea, to stay in office, and kicking us in the shins to demonstrate some superficial independence of us, or, as was the case in South Vietnam, a constant overthrow of governments as they became acknowledged to be American puppets.

When we go into a country and put our arms around somebody and say, "This is the leader who we want to be your president or your prime minister," no matter how popular they might be at the time, we put the political kiss of death on them. And the proud people who live in that country automatically react against a puppet. Had we spent another fifty thousand lives and had we spent another 150 billion dollars in South Vietnam and had we dropped the atomic bomb on North Vietnam, we still could not have propped up the governments of Thieu or Ky.

In the last two or three years, I've traveled as an official visitor to eleven foreign countries—in the Far East, the Mideast, South America, Central America, and Europe—and met with leaders there and talked to them at length. I've also been in our embassies. And I think in the recent administrations there has been a vivid demonstration of our attitude toward other people and our lack of respect for them in the quality of diplomatic officials appointed. When I go into an embassy in South America or Central America or Europe and see sitting as our ambassador, our representative there, a bloated, ignorant, rich major contributor to a presidential campaign who can't even speak the language of the country in which he serves, and who knows even less about our own country and our consciousness and our ideals and our motivation, it's an insult to me and to the people of America and to the people of that country.

Quite often this results in a devastating loss of respect for our nation. I doubt if you would find any diplomats in Washington who don't speak English. But you go into a small country that's embryonic or weak or dark-skinned, and you very seldom find an American diplomat who can even speak their language, and they know it. But you won't find a Japanese diplomat or a Russian diplomat or a German diplomat there who can't speak their language and who doesn't seem to care about them. And when you come to a recent disgraceful vote that took place at the United Nations, on Zionism, and think that we lacked seven votes; if we could have changed just seven votes we could have avoided that disgraceful act, and we lost such support as Brazil and Mexico and many others. Those ought to be our friends, but they feel we have neglected them and relegated them to secondary position of importance in the minds and hearts of the American people. The other nations of the world who think we ought to be leaders have lost respect for us. They don't think we tell the truth. We're not predictable. We don't respect them. And we've lost their respect for us.

The last thing I want to say is this: We have an inevitable role of leadership to play. Even if countries don't trust us and don't respect us at this moment because we're considered to be warlike, we're considered to be disrespectful of them, they still recognize that because of our innate political strength, the size of our country, our economic strength, our military strength, that we are going to be a major voice in the world, and we ought to assume that position. We can't withdraw from participation in the United Nations or its ancillary organizations, because that's where decisions are made which affect the lives of everyone who lives in Georgia or Kentucky or Iowa. In food, population, freedom of the seas, international trade, stable monetary systems, environmental quality, access to commodities and energy, and so forth, we've got to be part of it. But our foreign policy ought not be based on military might nor political power nor economic pressure. It ought to be based on the fact that we are right and decent and honest and truthful and predictable and respectful; in other words, that our foreign policy itself accurately represents the character and the ideals of the American people. But it doesn't. We have set a different standard of ethics and morality as a nation than we have in our own private lives as individuals who comprise the nation. And that ought to be changed. The President ought to be the spokesman for this country, not the Secretary of State. And when the President speaks, he ought to try to represent as accurately as he can what our people are. And that's the basis, I believe, on which a successful foreign policy can be based, to correct some of the defects we know about and to restore us around the world.

National Democratic Issues Conference
Louisville, Kentucky
November 23, 1975

Victory in New Hampshire

LET ME say just a few words to you. I think you know how close I feel to you, and to the people of New Hampshire and to the people of Oklahoma, the people of Iowa, the people of Maine.

I want to repair the damage that has been done to the relationship between our people and our government. And to tear down the walls that have separated us from it. And you are the ones that have made it possible for me to do it.

This Saturday, South Carolina. A week from today, Massachusetts.

And I hope that what we've done here in New Hampshire today will be a very good projection of how the New England people feel about me.

And then comes the big test, as you well know, when there's going to be a primary, and it's a two-man race in Florida the ninth of March. And we're going to take it—if I can just move Carter's army to Massachusetts and to Florida.

Let me introduce you to my secret weapons. First of all, my wife Rosalynn. My sons and their wives: Jack and Judy, Chip and Caron, Jeff and Annette.

Let me just say one more thing to you and then I want to come down and shake some hands if you don't mind. I want to shake hands with every one of you and thank you because you're just like part of my family. And I believe that when we get to the convention in July, after all the hard work, there's going to be a very quick decision. I think, first ballot.

Rally
Manchester, New Hampshire
February 24, 1976

73

The Dreams of the Common People

IN A political campaign you acquire delegate votes and popular support and now—according to some of the polls, the Gallup and others—I'm at the top of the list in support from the people. I've come in first in eleven states that have chosen delegates, and I think our campaign has been a growing one, and a successful one. And that's an important aspect of the electoral process. Another thing that is acquired is a knowledge of the people concerning me—my character, strengths, weaknesses, and my stands on every conceivable issue.

The other thing you derive from a campaign is a knowledge of our nation, what it is and what it ought to be. You become a repository of ideas and suggestions and complaints and criticisms, hopes, dreams, frustrations, ideals, aspirations. You form an intimate relationship with voters, an intimacy that needs to be carried over after the election into the White House so that the people of our country don't feel alienated from or excluded from our government, so we no longer feel as though we are outsiders, particularly those who are poor, disadvantaged, rural, illiterate, without influence, who belong to minority groups, who very rarely have an opportunity to express themselves in strong terms as a nation's policies are shaped, because quite often the policies are shaped, the decisions are made, by people who are powerful enough and rich enough and influential enough and prominent enough not to suffer personally when governmental mistakes are made. So a President has to be one who speaks for those who have no adequate spokesman. . . .

My first political responsibility was on a local library board. I was put on the board because I checked out more books than anyone else in the county. My library card number is number five in Sumter County. For I remember that I started reading books as an isolated country boy when I was very young. I had a superintendent named Miss Julia Coleman who encouraged me to do so.

One of the first books that she recommended to me, after I had finished a list of classical volumes, was *War and Peace*. She used to give a silver star for every five books, a gold star for every ten; and she finally said, "Jimmy, I think you're ready now"—I was about twelve years old—"to read *War and Peace*." And I breathed a sigh of relief because after all those classical books I thought I was finally going to read something about cowboys and Indians; but when I went to the library and checked the book out, I was stricken because it was 1450 pages thick.

But that book I've read several times since then. And, as you know, it is a story about Napoleon, who went into Russia hoping to be the conqueror of the world, completely confident. But he underestimated two things: the love of the peasant for his land and the severity of the Russian winter. And to make a long story short, he retreated in defeat. The course of human events was changed. But the book is not about Napoleon or the Czar of Russia. It is about the common ordinary people—barbers, housewives, privates in the army, farmers, and others—and the point that Tolstoy makes is that the course of human events, even the greatest historical events, are controlled and shaped not by the leaders of the nations but by the combined hopes and dreams and aspirations and courage and conviction of the common ordinary people. And if that's true in a nation like Russia with a czar, or France with an emperor, how much more true is it in our own country? For under the Constitution of the United States we are guaranteed not only the right but the duty to let our own individual aspirations, trust, moral judgment, character, shape our government. I believe we have a nation that will respond to that kind of public sentiment and public involvement.

I intend to be the President. I think I have a good chance to win, but it is no more my country than it is yours. If there are things you don't like about our nation, if we've made mistakes that you'd like never to see made again, if there are divisions among our people that you would like to see healed, if there are hopes and dreams in your own lives that you would like to see realized, or in the lives of your children, I hope that you will take advantage of this year, election year, and help guarantee in the future that our country actively represents the finest aspects of our people and prove to the rest of the world—that is very important, but more important to prove to our own people—that we still live in the greatest nation on earth.

City Club
Cleveland, Ohio
April 8, 1976

The Country Changed

THE PRESIDENCY is a very important office. I remember how Richard Nixon came in the White House in '68, when the Kennedy and Johnson administrations were over. The Congress didn't change. But the country changed. The day the President changed, the country changed. And the poor people and the black people and the uneducated people and the rural people and the sick people and the old people felt that they lost something. And the thing they had lost was hope. Because they didn't have a strong voice anymore to speak for them, and to search out discrimination and unfairness and the needless human suffering, and to give people the pride of having a job.

One of the worst things you can do to somebody is to take away their right to let their own lives be meaningful. God only gave us one life to live, with a certain amount of talent and ability; and for a person to say, "My life is being wasted because I don't have a job," is a devastating blow. So the country changed when the President changed.

Our nation is best served by a strong President, independent, aggressive, working with a strong and independent Congress.

In the absence of leadership, the country drifts. But I want to be sure that the President, if I'm elected, is not a proud person, not an isolated person, not one that separates himself from you. I want to be a good President. I won't be any better President than I am a candidate. And the intimacy that I form this year, between myself as the candidate and you as voters, is the same kind of closeness that I want to see as President when I am in the White House.

UAW Breakfast
Washington, D.C.
April 13, 1976

"Ethnic Purity"

On April 4, 1976, the New York *Daily News* carried an article on Carter which included in the sixteenth paragraph this remark: "Asked about low income, scatter-site housing in the suburbs, Carter replied, 'I see nothing wrong with ethnic purity being maintained. I would not force a racial integration of a neighborhood by government action. But I would not permit discrimination against a family moving into the neighborhood.'" A few days later a controversy arose over Carter's use of the term "ethnic purity." Carter eventually apologized for using the expression, and on April 13 made the following remarks to a group of editors and reporters.

Q. Governor, I'd like to ask you, maybe get it over with, the question about your "ethnic purity" remark. You're an introspective man, you had a chance to go back to the farm this weekend and do some thinking. Have you reviewed the use of those words and come up with some kind of an idea in your own mind of what led you to use those words?
A. I had no idea that the phrase would be obnoxious to people as it was. I noticed that President Ford has used the words "ethnic treasure," and I myself have substituted the words "ethnic character," "ethnic heritage," but I don't have any apology to make for my position on housing. I don't know anything I can do except apologize, which I already have, to those who were offended by the use of the word "purity."

I think I've spelled out my position very definitively. When you have a neighbor with an ethnic character, I think that is a very proud possession of our country and don't think that the federal government ought to deliberately destroy that character, but I would insist avidly on the rigid enforcement of open housing legislation. I passed such legislation as Governor. When federal funds are spent, in public housing or for other reasons in housing, then I would favor the affirmative action programs that insure that families with different ethnic backgrounds, and also different economic status, would be given a right in any major neighborhood for access housing.

American Society of Newspaper Editors
Washington, D.C.
April 13, 1976

I Believe in a Strong Defense

You all sit down, please. In about nine or ten months you can all stand up when I'm introduced.

It's really a pleasure to be back in Texas. You've had both the foresight and the friendship toward me to give me your advice and counsel and political and financial support now for a number of months before many people knew that I had a chance to win. And I'll always be grateful to you for this confidence that you have expressed in me.

We finished the first phase of the campaign Tuesday in Pennsylvania. A phase that we laid out almost three and a half years ago—and I have to admit to you that it ended sooner than I expected—and that was the phase of elimination of my major opponents. At first when we decided to run, I thought it would be Senator Kennedy and Governor Wallace. And later, as you know, Kennedy withdrew and Walter Mondale got in the race, and then later it was Birch Bayh and Congressman Udall and Senator Jackson and more recently Senator Humphrey, some very fine, fine men who entered the race, and we've now come out ahead of all of them. It is very difficult at this point to see who will continue in a strong way in opposition to me.

I really had thought that all the way through the California, Ohio, and New Jersey primaries on the eighth of June that I would have at least one major opponent and that the issue between myself and that opponent would be in doubt. But I think that Pennsylvania, because of an extraordinary amount of outpouring of help that came in there from all over the nation, the victory was so great that, although Jackson and Udall might continue on, I think that for all practical purposes they have no chance to win.

I don't say that in an arrogant fashion, or an overconfident way. I think that if there is one mistake that could cost me the election, it would be the taking of people for granted. I want to keep the intimate, personal, close relationship between myself, as the candidate, and the voters of this nation, all the way through the entire process. And I want to carry that same relationship over into the White House when I am President, if that should be my lot. I want to be just as close to you then as I am this morning.

I believe in a strong defense. The number one priority of any President has got to be the security of our country, the safety of our country.

I spent eleven years in the Navy, most of the time in submarines. I'm a graduate of Annapolis. . . . I worked under Admiral Hyman Rickover, and he was a very stern instructor and boss. He still considers himself to be my boss, and I can't get away from the feeling myself. I don't know how I'm going to feel when I'm President and he's just a four-star admiral. But I do know the importance of a strong and adequate defense. The defense mechanism is very wasteful and there's a lot of pent-up hope among the leaders in our Pentagon that we can make it efficient and economical and purposeful. It now does everything in God's world. Everything that civilian agencies do, the Defense Department tries to do also. Admiral Rickover has twenty-one different intermediate levels of authority between himself and the Secretary of Defense, which is an unbelievable conglomerate and confused bureaucracy in itself. We've got too many military bases overseas, about two thousand. We've got twice as many support troops per combat troop as the Soviet Union does. For every instructor in the military, we've got less than two students, and so forth. A lot of things need to be corrected. But in the process, we would have a much more tough, simple, well-organized fighting force. The only function of the military ought to be to be able to fight. And in that capability rests the assurance that we won't have to fight.

I need the help of people like you in this room. I'll try to make sure that every time I speak, it is openly.

I don't have any obligations to anyone, except an obligation to individual persons in this nation for their confidence in me. I intend to go into the White House that way. I'm not going to bind myself with any sort of private agreements to anybody and that will include appointments or Cabinet posts or judgeships or ambassadorships or to special-interest groups no matter how benevolent they might be.

We have in this room this morning one of the most benevolent, farsighted, hardworking, honest, intelligent, productive groups that exist in the whole nation. And that is the producers of peanuts. And even to these fine gentlemen, I wouldn't make any private promises.

Reception
Dallas, Texas
April 30, 1976

The Essence of a Worthwhile Life

During the hard-fought Maryland primary, Governor Edmund Brown of California criticized Governor Carter's proposals for government reorganization and for zero-based budgeting. Governor Brown's own statements seemed to call for a more passive approach to government, and to suggest that it might be best to let government "drift" for a while. The following is part of a reply Governor Carter made to Governor Brown's criticisms.

A BASIC issue has been raised in this campaign. Do we need to reorganize the federal government? I say the answer is yes; my opponent here in Maryland says no.

He has said that the waste, inefficiency, and insensitivity of the federal government are not the fault of the system but of the people who are trying to make that system work— that "it's not the boxes but the people who are in them."

That is wrong. I have seen at first hand that most government employees want to do a good job. When I reorganized the government of Georgia, our merit system employees were some of my strongest supporters. They are not perfect, but they are certainly as conscientious and dedicated as the average worker anywhere else. . . .

It has been said zero-based budgeting will not work, that it is a phony issue—because they tried it for two or three weeks in California and gave up.

It worked in Georgia—because we made it work. Of course, it took a year instead of three weeks, but we were able to cut fifty million dollars from the budget at the end of that year, so I think it was worth it.

In the years ahead, the Presidency requires more than philosophical inquiries issued from above the battle. The Presidency will require leadership and answers. It will require that the President place himself in the thick of battle for reform of a disgraceful tax system, an unworkable budgetary process, a wasteful bureaucracy, and an antiquated judicial system.

What is at the heart of the matter is how we look at the world around us. There are those who believe that it is not worthwhile to try—that life just is and you float along with it, that human nature never changes and human beings are unable to improve the conditions of mankind, that it is futile to set any goals for ourselves or our nation.

I could not disagree more strongly. I believe that the very essence of a worthwhile life is in the striving. I do not fear the possibility of failure so much as the resigned acceptance of what is mediocre or wrong.

I believe that what we as individuals do or fail to do can make a difference for ourselves and for others.

I know that the institutions of this world will always be imperfect, but I will always insist that we can do better.

Those who dispute the ability of men and women to improve the lot of mankind have never seen the impact of REA on the life of a small boy in the rural South.

They are unfamiliar with the meaning of a hot lunch to a child of the ghetto.

They naively deny the true meaning of the lives of a Jefferson, a Lincoln, an FDR, or a Martin Luther King.

They fail to comprehend what the conquest of polio, diphtheria, yellow fever, or malaria has meant to people all over the globe.

I have seen the guarantee of the right to vote alter the politics of a region.

I have seen a community mental health center change the life of a retarded child and her family.

I have seen the opportunity for training and a decent job break the cycle of two generations of dependence and despair.

There are difficult times ahead. But we have faced difficult times before and we have prevailed. We have prevailed because we dared to dream great dreams, because we refused to be content with injustice and mediocrity, because we were willing to try.

I seek the highest political office in the world—the Presidency of the United States. I cannot promise that you will always agree with me. I cannot promise that I will always be right. I can promise that I will never be satisfied with less than the best, that I will never stop trying to make it better.

Reply to Governor Brown
Rockville, Maryland
May 1976

Interview with Bill Moyers

MOYERS: When you were growing up in that wooden clapboard house on that dusty road, spearing fish in your spare time, or netting fish in your spare time, did you ever think about being President?

CARTER: No. I didn't have but one desire, aspiration, that I can remember, and that is going to the Naval Academy. Nobody in my father's family had ever finished high school before I did, and to actually go to college, in itself, was a notable goal to establish in our family.

MOYERS: I've been intrigued as to why you almost suddenly gave up your military career and went back to Plains. Your father died. And you thought about his life, and you went back—but was there something else?

CARTER: Well, up until that time I guess I was a naval officer who enjoyed my work. I had the best jobs in the Navy.

And then my father had terminal cancer, and I had to go home to be with him about the last month of his life. I hadn't known him since I was about seventeen years old. This was ten, twelve years later.

And I had always wanted, I guess, ultimately to be the Chief of Naval Operations, which is, you know, it's top of the Navy. But when I went back home to where I had lived and saw what my father's life meant—in the view of those who knew him best—his service on the school board, his working for a new hospital, his dealing with the education of farmers who bought seed and so forth from him, his life in the church and his life in politics. He'd just been elected to the Legislature and served one year when he died.

Well, I could see then a pull on me that was almost irresistible to go back and re-cement my ties to my birthplace.

But I had a choice to make. Did I want to be the Chief of Naval Operations and devote my whole life to that one narrowly defined career, which was a good one, or did I want to go back and build a more diverse life with a lot of friends, permanence, stability, in a community, in a relationship, in the life of a whole group of people? And I chose the latter. But I've never regretted a day that I served in the Navy.

MOYERS: What do you think it did for you or to you? Did it stamp this discipline that everyone tells me about? This respect for authority?

CARTER: Yes, I think so. Obviously, the Naval Academy is quite heavily disciplined. And a life on a ship—particularly as a junior officer—is a heavy discipline; to move in the submarines is a heavier discipline. And then I met Rickover, who knew me as one of his maybe four young naval officers who had come in on the *Seawolf* and the *Nautilus*, which were the two submarines that were built with atomic power. And he demanded from me a standard of performance and a depth of commitment that I had never realized before that I could achieve. And I think, second to my own father, Admiral Rickover had more effect on my life than any other man.

MOYERS: Can you step back as the civilian Commander-in-Chief from this heavy influence of the military and of an admiral in your life?

CARTER: I can.

MOYERS: Can you?

CARTER: Yes, yes. There's no aspect of a militaristic inclination now on my part. I feel free of that completely. But the self-discipline has stuck with me. I have a constant drive just to do the best I can, and sometimes it's disconcerting to other people, but it's not an unpleasant thing for me. I don't feel that I've got to win. I feel a sense of equanimity about it. If I do my best and lose, I don't have any regrets.

MOYERS: What drives you?

CARTER: I don't know exactly how to express it. As I said, it's not an unpleasant sense of being driven. I feel like I have one life to live. I feel like that God wants me to do the best I can with it. And that's quite often my major prayer. Let me live my life so that it will be meaningful. And I enjoy attacking difficult problems and solving solutions and answering the difficult questions and the meticulous organization of a complicated effort. It's a challenge—possibly it's like a game. I don't know. I don't want to lower it by saying it's just a "game," but it's an enjoyable thing for me.

MOYERS: How do you know—this is a question I hear from a lot of young people—how do you know God's will?

CARTER: Well, I pray frequently. And not continually, but many times a day. When I have a sense of peace and just self-assurance—I don't know where it comes from—that what I'm doing is the right thing, I assume, maybe in an unwarranted way, that that's doing God's will.

MOYERS: Let's go back a minute to the people who touched you when you were young. Who else?

CARTER: Well, there were two women in particular when I was young. One, obviously, was my mother. I'm much more like my mother than I am my father. She read day and night, at the breakfast table, the lunch table, the supper table. I do, still. She was very compassionate.

MOYERS: You mean she read out loud?

CARTER: No, no. No, she just read books. And so did I, by the way. My father didn't. He read the newspaper and maybe *News and World Report,* and that was just about it. Mother always was a champion of disadvantaged people. In our area it was poor whites and all blacks. Later, when she was past retirement age, she, as you know, went to India for two years and she, I think, she came back when she was after seventy.

MOYERS: The Peace Corps?

CARTER: In the Peace Corps, yes. In the Peace Corps. But she's always been that way. Miss Julia Coleman was a superintendent of our school when I was growing up in Plains. Plains is a town of about six hundred population. The schoolhouse is still there. And she saw something in me, I think, when I was a little child, a hunger to learn, and although I lived in a rural area, three or four miles, three miles from Plains. We didn't have electricity or running water. But we didn't suffer. But she made sure that I listened to classical music. She would make me do it. And she'd make sure that I learned the famous paintings and the authors and the artists, and she gave me lists of books to read, and she was very strict with me.

MOYERS: You said once that you never really seriously considered disobeying your father. And I wonder if anyone who never disobeyed his father can understand the rest of us.

CARTER [Laughter]: Well, as a matter of fact, I never disobeyed my father in that when he said, Jimmy, you do something, I failed to do it. But on many occasions I did things that I knew my father didn't like, and I was punished very severely because of it.

In fact, my father very seldom gave me an order. If all the other field workers were off for the afternoon, and he wanted me to turn the potato vines so they could be plowed Monday morning, Daddy would say to me—He called me "Hot."

MOYERS: He called you what?

CARTER: "Hot"—"Hotshot"—is what he called me. He says, "Hot, would you like to turn the potato vines this afternoon?" And I would much rather go to the movie or something. But I always said, "Yes, sir, Daddy, I would." And I would do it. But he didn't have to give me many direct orders. But I never did disobey a direct order my father gave me.

MOYERS: Was it a stern life?

CARTER: Yes, it was a stern life. But there wasn't much to do. [Laughter.] If it hadn't been a stern life— We didn't have any movies in Plains, and I remember that when I was a small child we had a very small bowling alley that was not nearly as long as a regular one was, but it was an exciting thing for Plains when we had a bowling alley for a while, with the small balls.

But my life was spent in a fairly isolated way, out in the woods and in the streams and swamps and fields.

MOYERS: What do you do now for fun?

CARTER: I read a lot, and about the only thing that I do for fun now is to look forward to being home. I stay gone a lot, away from Plains, away from our house, away from our little daughter, away from my wife, away from my mother, away from my mother-in-law, my brother and sister and my wife's kinfolks. And when I get home, I change immediately into work clothes, put on brogans and dungarees, and either go to the farm or walk in the woods. My wife and I hunt arrowheads. We go out into the fields after they've been plowed and rained on, and we walk, sometimes for hours, just talking to each other about different things, sometimes politics, quite often about our family. We have very few moments alone. And so the fun in my life now is just re-establishing for a twenty-four-hour period, or thirty-two-hour period, whatever it is, the structure of my family.

MOYERS: What do you think we're on earth for?

CARTER: I don't know. I could quote the Biblical references to creation, that God created us in His own image, hoping that we'd be perfect, and we turned out to be not perfect but very sinful. And then when Christ was asked what are the two great commandments from God which should direct our lives, He said, "To love God with all your heart and soul and mind, and love your neighbor as yourself." So I try to take that condensation of the Christian theology and let it be something through which I search for a meaningful existence. I don't worry about it too much anymore. I used to when I was a college sophomore, and we used to debate for hours and hours about why we're here, who made us, where shall we go, what's our purpose.

MOYERS: Do you ever have any doubts? People say to me, "Jimmy Carter appears to be so full of certainty and conviction." Do you ever have any doubts? About yourself, about God, about life?

CARTER: I can't think of any, you know. Obviously I don't know all of the answers to the philosophical questions and teleological questions that—you know, the questions that are contrived. But the things that I haven't been able to answer in a theory of supposition, I just accept them and go on. The things that I can't influence or change.

I do have, obviously, many doubts about the best way to answer a question or how to alleviate a concern or how to meet a need. Or how to—how to create in my own life a more meaningful purpose and to let my life be expanded in my heart and mind. So doubt about the best avenue to take among many options is a kind of doubt. That is a constant presence with me. But doubt about my faith? No. Doubt about my purpose in life? I don't have any doubts about that.

MOYERS: Governor, when you say that, when you say, "I will never lie, I will never mislead you," people have more doubts about your perception of reality than they do about your integrity.

CARTER: I understand.

MOYERS: Other people are not saying, "Jimmy Carter is trying to put one over on us," but "Jimmy Carter just doesn't understand the way Washington and international power works."

CARTER: I understand that. And I have thought about that a lot, because I've been in debate a lot, and one of the great surprises to me in the campaign was that when I made that simple statement eighteen months ago—not in a—not in a fervent way, not even in a way to surprise anybody, that I, as a candidate and as a President, I'm not going to lie to you, that it became so controversial.

MOYERS: Why were you surprised?

CARTER: I was surprised that it was a controversy. I— The first time I ever voted was in 1948. I was in submarine school. All the other officers there voted for Dewey. I voted for Truman. He's still my favorite President. I don't believe that Truman ever told me a lie or told the American people a lie. May have. I don't believe he did. I think other presidents since then have. I don't see any reason for it.

If I'm elected, at the end of four years or eight years I hope people will say, "You know, Jimmy Carter made a lot of mistakes, but he never told me a lie."

MOYERS: You're saying, in effect, "Trust me. I will do those things."

CARTER: Yes.

MOYERS: Is that right?

CARTER: Yes.

MOYERS: And there's no question but that you have tapped a feeling in the country that wants to trust.

CARTER: Yes.

MOYERS: Are you aware that once you become President you will be making decisions that will immediately make some people unhappy who thought they saw in you a champion? Isn't that inevitable?

CARTER: Yes.

MOYERS: Well, what do you do about that disillusionment? And don't they then say, "Well, Jimmy Carter's not trustworthy"?

CARTER: I can't answer that question. . . .

The ones who cling to me as a friend are the ones who throughout their whole lives have been deprived of an opportunity to make decisions about their own lives. I saw clearly as Governor of Georgia, I see clearly now as a prospective, possible President, that in almost every instance people who make decisions in government that affect human beings very seldom suffer when their decisions are wrong. The people who carved out a disgraceful, wasteful, confused, overlapping welfare system, their families never draw welfare. The people who carved out a disgraceful tax system, they don't ever get hurt, because they're cared for when the tax laws are written.

The criminal justice system—I'm not a lawyer. We pride ourselves in having a good, fair criminal justice system. It's not fair. Now wealth is a major factor in whether or not you get justice or not.

MOYERS: Do you think this is a just society?

CARTER: No, no, I don't. I think one of the major responsibilities I have as a leader and as a potential leader is to try to establish justice. And that applies to a broad gamut of things—international affairs, peace, equality, elimination of injustice in racial discrimination, elimination of injustice in tax programs, elimination of injustice in our criminal justice system, and so forth. And it's not a crusade. It's just common sense.

MOYERS: You're going to be an activist President?

CARTER: I am.

MOYERS: What do you think the purpose of government is?

CARTER: To provide legitimate services to our people; to help preserve peace; to provide a mechanism by which the people's character can be expressed in international affairs. I think the purpose of government is to alleviate inequities. I think the purpose of government is to provide for things that we can't provide ourselves.

MOYERS: Let me go back to some personal questions as we close here. You said once that you were strongly influenced by a sermon whose title was "If You Were Arrested for Being a Christian, Would There Be Enough Evidence to Convict You?" What is the evidence that the rest of us can see of a Christian?

CARTER: I don't know. That's a hard question to answer, because I don't think I'm better than anyone else. . . .

I was going through a state in my life then that was a very

difficult one. I had run for Governor and lost. Everything I did was not gratifying. When I succeeded in something, it was a horrible experience for me. And I thought I was a good Christian. I was the chairman of the board of deacons. I was the head of the brotherhood in all the thirty-four churches in my district, and head of the finance committee, and Sunday School teacher just about all my life. I thought I really was a good Christian.

And one day the preacher gave this sermon. I just remember the title which you described—"If You Were Arrested for Being a Christian, Would There Be Any Evidence to Convict You?"

And my answer by the time that sermon was over was no. I never had really committed myself totally to God. My Christian beliefs were superficial, based on pride. I'd never done much for other people. I was always thinking about myself, and I changed somewhat for the better. I formed a much more intimate relationship with Christ. And since then I've had just about like a new life. As far as hatreds, frustrations, I feel at ease with myself. And it doesn't mean that I'm better, but I'm better off myself.

MOYERS: What do you pray for?

CARTER: I ask God to let me do what's right. And to let me do what's best—that my life be meaningful, in an optimum way. And, if I win or lose, I believe I can accept the decision with composure and without regrets, or without animosities or hatreds or deep disappointment even.

MOYERS: In your own search for what Tillich said is the truth about man's relationships to man and to God?

CARTER: Yes.

MOYERS: What's the most significant discovery Jimmy Carter has made?

CARTER: Well, I think I described it superficially a while ago. I think it affected my life more than anything else. This is embarrassing a little bit for me to talk about it, because it's personal, but in my relationship with Christ and with God, I became able in the process to look at it in practical terms, to accept defeat, to get pleasure out of successes, to be at peace with a world. For instance, one of the things that I derived from it is that when I stand on a factory shift line, like I did this morning in Erie, Pennsylvania, the General Electric plant, everybody that comes through there, when I shake hands with them, for that instant, I really care about them. In a genuine way. And I believe they know it.

Quite often I will shake hands with a woman who works in a plant, say, an older woman, and I'll just touch her hand, and quite frequently they'll put their arms around my neck and say, you know, "God bless you, son." Or "Good luck. I'll help you. Good luck." It's kind of a relationship with people around me, but I don't want to insinuate that I'm better than other people. I've still got a long way to go, but you asked me a difficult question.

MOYERS: But you care, though. You do—

CARTER: I care.

MOYERS: —you have found that you care about people?

CARTER: I do.

MOYERS: I was going to ask you if you saw the President as a pastor to 230 million people.

CARTER: I don't look on the Presidency with religious connotations. But it gives me a chance to serve, and it also gives me a chance to magnify whatever influence I have—either for good or bad, and I hope it will be for the good.

MOYERS: Gives you power, too?

CARTER: And power . . .

MOYERS: You have been searching for power for the last ten years?

CARTER: I can't deny it.

MOYERS: You ran four years for the governorship, and been running two years for the Presidency. Do you need power?

CARTER: Well, I think so. That it is an unfulfilled, all-obsessive hunger—no. I feel powerful enough now. And secure enough now. Wealthy enough now. I have a good family life now. I've got a lot of blessings that would give me a good life for the rest of my days. But I would like to have a chance to change things that I don't like, and to correct the inequities as I discern them, and to be a strong spokesman for those that are not strong. And I guess that's power. So I can't deny that one of the purposes that I want to be President is to have power, yes.

Public Broadcasting Service
May 6, 1976

Nuclear Energy and World Order

I HAVE had training as a nuclear engineer, working in the United States Navy on our country's early nuclear submarine program. I learned how nuclear power can be used for peaceful purposes—for propelling ships, for generating electric power, and for scientific and medical research. I am acutely aware of its potential, and its dangers. Once I helped in disassembling a damaged nuclear reactor core in an experimental reactor at Chalk River, Canada.

From my experience in the Navy and more recently as Governor of Georgia, I have come to certain basic conclusions about the energy problem. The world has only enough oil to last about thirty to forty years at the present rate of consumption. It has large coal reserves, with perhaps two hundred years of reserves in the United States alone. The United States must shift from oil to coal, taking care about the environmental problems involved in coal production and use. Our country must also maintain strict energy conservation measures, and derive increasing amounts of energy from renewable sources such as the sun.

U.S. dependence on nuclear power should be kept to the minimum necessary to meet our needs. We should apply much stronger safety standards as we regulate its use. And we must be honest with our people concerning its problems and dangers.

I recognize that many other countries of the world do not have the fossil fuel reserves of the United States. With the fourfold increase in the price of oil, many countries have concluded that they have no immediate alternative except to concentrate on nuclear power.

But all of us must recognize that the widespread use of nuclear power brings many risks. Power reactors may malfunction and cause widespread radiological damage, unless stringent safety requirements are met. Radioactive wastes may be a menace to future generations and civilizations, unless they are effectively isolated within the biosphere forever. And terrorists or other criminals may steal plutonium and make weapons to threaten society or its political leaders with nuclear violence, unless strict security measures are developed and implemented to prevent nuclear theft.

Beyond these dangers, there is the fearsome prospect that the spread of nuclear reactors will mean the spread of nuclear weapons to many nations. By 1990, the developing nations alone will produce enough plutonium in their reactors to build three thousand Hiroshima-size bombs a year, and by the year 2000, worldwide plutonium production may be over one million pounds a year—the equivalent of a hundred thousand bombs a year, about half of it outside of the United States.

We need new international action to limit the spread of nuclear weapons.

In the past, public attention has been focused on the problem of controlling the escalation of the strategic nuclear weapons capabilities among an increasing number of nations.

And yet the danger to world peace may be as great, if not greater, if this second effort of control should fail. The more countries that possess nuclear weapons, the greater the risk that nuclear warfare might erupt in local conflicts, and the greater the danger that these could trigger a major nuclear war.

To date, the principal instrument of control has been the Nonproliferation Treaty which entered into force in 1970.

By 1976, ninety-five non-weapons states had ratified the Treaty, including the advanced industrial states of Western Europe, and prospectively of Japan. In so doing, these nations agreed not to develop nuclear weapons or explosives. In addition they agreed to accept international safeguards on all their peaceful nuclear activities, developed by themselves or with outside assistance, under agreements negotiated with the International Atomic Energy Agency—a little-appreciated but an unprecedented step forward, in the development of international law.

Important as this achievement is, it cannot be a source of complacency, particularly under present circumstances. There are still a dozen or more important countries with active nuclear power programs which have not joined the Treaty. Hopefully, some of these may decide to become members; but in the case of several of them, this is unlikely until the underlying tensions behind their decision to maintain a nuclear weapons option are resolved.

The NPT was not conceived of as a one-way street. Under the Treaty, in return for the commitments of the non-weapons states, a major undertaking of the nuclear weapons states (and other nuclear suppliers in a position to do so) was to provide special nuclear power benefits to Treaty members, particularly to developing countries.

The advanced countries have not done nearly enough in providing such peaceful benefits to convince the member states that they are better off inside the Treaty than outside.

In fact, recent commercial transactions by some of the supplier countries have conferred special benefits on non-Treaty members, thereby largely removing any incentive for such recipients to join the Treaty. They consider themselves better off outside. Furthermore, while individual facilities in these non-Treaty countries may be subject to international safeguards, others may not be; and India has demonstrated that such facilities may provide the capability to produce nuclear weapons.

As a further part of the two-way street, there is an obligation by the nuclear weapons states under the Treaty to pursue negotiations in good faith to reach agreement to control and reduce the nuclear arms race.

We Americans must be honest about the problems of proliferation of nuclear weapons. Our nuclear deterrent remains an essential element of world order in this area. Nevertheless, by enjoining sovereign nations to forgo nuclear weapons, we are asking for a form of self-denial that we have not been able to accept ourselves.

I believe we have little right to ask others to deny themselves such weapons for the indefinite future unless we demonstrate meaningful progress toward the goal of control, then reduction, and ultimately elimination of nuclear arsenals.

Unfortunately, the agreements reached to date have succeeded largely in changing the buildup in strategic arms from a "quantitative" to a "qualitative" arms race. It is time in the SALT talks that we complete the stage of agreeing on ceilings and get down to the centerpiece of SALT—the actual negotiation of reductions in strategic forces, and measures effectively halting the race in strategic weapons technology. The world is waiting, but not necessarily for long. The longer effective arms reduction is postponed, the more likely it is that other nations will be encouraged to develop their own nuclear capability.

There is one step that can be taken at once. The United States and the Soviet Union should conclude an agreement prohibiting all nuclear explosions for a period of five years, whether they be weapons tests or so-called peaceful nuclear explosions, and encourage all other countries to join. At the end of the five-year period the agreement can be continued if it serves the interest of the parties.

I am aware of the Soviet objections to a comprehensive treaty that does not allow peaceful nuclear explosions. I also remember, during the Kennedy administration, when the roles were reversed. Then the U.S. had a similar proposal that permitted large-scale peaceful explosions. However, in order to reach an accord, we withdrew our proposal. Similarly, today, if the U.S. really pushed a comprehensive test ban treaty, I believe the United States and the world commuity could persuade the USSR to dispose of this issue and accept a comprehensive test ban.

The nonproliferation significance of the superpowers' decision to ban peaceful nuclear explosions would be very great because of its effect on countries who have resisted the Nonproliferation Treaty's prohibition of "peaceful" nuclear explosives, even though they are indistinguishable from bombs.

A comprehensive test ban would also signal to the world the determination of the signatory states to call a halt to the further development of nuclear weaponry. It has been more than a decade since the Limited Test Ban Treaty entered into force, and well over a hundred nations are not parties to that agreement.

It now appears that the United States and the Soviet Union are close to an agreement that would prohibit underground nuclear tests above 150 kilotons. This so-called threshold test ban treaty represents a wholly inadequate step beyond the limited test ban. We can and should do more. Our national verification capabilities in the last twenty years have advanced to the point where we no longer have to rely on on-site inspection to distinguish between earthquakes and even very small weapons tests.

Finally, such a treaty would not only be a demonstration on the part of the superpowers to agree to limit their own weapons development. As President Kennedy foresaw in 1963, the most important objective of a comprehensive treaty of universal application would be its inhibiting effect on the spread of nuclear weapons by prohibiting tests by every signatory state.

Of one thing I am certain, the hour is too late for business as usual, for politics as usual, or for diplomacy as usual. An alliance for survival is needed—transcending regions and ideologies—if we are to assure mankind a safe passage to the twenty-first century.

The United Nations
New York, New York
May 13, 1976

The Issue Is Faith

... I THINK that the political campaign this year is operating on two levels.

On one level we have the tangible issues—unemployment, welfare, taxation—but on another level we have the intangible issue of the cynicism and apathy that afflict too many of our fellow Americans.

Our people have been through too much. They have been lied to and cheated and tricked and bullied and confused and ignored, and they have finally had enough.

They are crying out not for government that is liberal or conservative or ideologically pure, but just honest and effective and compassionate.

If I had to sum up in one word what this campaign is all about, the word would be "faith."

The American people want to have faith in their government. And it is our responsibility, as public men and women, to do everything in our power to help them regain the faith that they have lost.

Let me close by saying to you what I have said to audiences all over America in the past sixteen months. All I want is the same thing you want. To have a nation with a government that is as good and honest and decent and competent and compassionate and as filled with love as are the American people.

California State Senate
Sacramento, California
May 20, 1976

I See an America . . .

Carter first used his "I see an America" peroration in this speech. It was later incorporated in his television advertising, his remarks at the Martin Luther King Hospital, and in his acceptance speech.

WE HAVE seen this campaign come full circle now, from "Jimmy Who?" to "Stop Carter!" The people who ignored me then are opposing me now, but mine is still the same campaign it was a year ago when I traveled alone and spoke in living rooms and meeting halls in Iowa and Florida and New Hampshire and every other state.

It is still the one campaign that speaks to and for the average hardworking, taxpaying American. It is still the one campaign with enough faith in the people of this country to take its case directly to all the people in all the states so the people could choose their President directly.

Ours is the campaign tied closely and intimately with working Americans on issues important to our lives. I have gone to the people with my positions on every basic issue facing this nation—tax reform, health, welfare reform, the environment, jobs, government reorganization, honesty in government—and in state after state the people have endorsed my positions with their votes.

My critics don't want to stop Carter. They want to stop the reforms I am committed to. They want to stop the people of this country from regaining control of their government. They want to preserve the status quo, to preserve politics as usual, to maintain at all costs their own entrenched, unresponsive, bankrupt, irresponsible political power.

They know I do not believe in business as usual or politics

103

as usual or a blind acceptance of the status quo. I am running for President because I have a vision of a new America, a different America, a better America, and it is not shared by those who are trying so hard to stop my campaign.

I have a vision of an America that is, in Bob Dylan's phrase, busy being born—not dying!

I see an America that is poised not only at the brink of a new century but at the dawn of a new era of responsive, responsible government.

I see an America that has turned her back on scandals and corruption and official cynicism and has finally demanded a government that deserves the trust and respect of her people.

I see an America with a tax system that does not cheat the average wage earner and with a government that is responsive to its people and with a system of justice that is even-handed to all.

I see a government that does not spy on its citizens but respects your dignity and your privacy and your right to be let alone.

I see an America in which "law and order" is not a slogan but a way of life, because our people have chosen to bind up our wounds and live in harmony.

I see an America in which your child and my child and every child, regardless of its background, receives an education that will permit full development of their talents and abilities.

I see an America that has a job for every man and woman who wants to work.

I see an America that will reconcile its need for new energy sources with its need for clean air, clean water, and an environment we can pass on with pride to our children and their children.

I see an American foreign policy that is as consistent and generous as the American people and that can once again be a beacon for the hopes of the entire world.

I see an America on the move again, united, its wounds healed, its head high, an America with pride in its past and faith in its future, moving into its third century with confidence and compassion, an America that lives up to the nobility of its Constitution and the decency of its people.

I see an America with a President who does not govern by vetoes and negativism but with vigor and vision and positive, affirmative, aggressive leadership.

This is my vision of America. It is one that reflects the deepest feelings of millions of people who have supported me this year. It is from you that I take my strength and my hope and my courage as I carry forth my campaign toward its ultimate success.

AFL-CIO Convention
Cincinnati, Ohio
May 27, 1976

The Prospect of Being President

PERHAPS SOME of you saw the reports yesterday of a CBS/ New York *Times* poll that said I was the only Democratic presidential contender running ahead of President Ford.

Obviously that news, coming near the end of my long quest for the Democratic nomination, is good news to me, but it is more than that. For me, as for you or for any person, the prospect of being President of the United States is a sobering thought, one that calls more for humility than for pride, more for reflection than for celebration.

I have never claimed to be better or wiser than any other person. I think my greatest strength is that I am an ordinary man, just like all of you, one who has worked and learned and loved his family and made mistakes and tried to correct them, without always succeeding.

Perhaps my campaign would not have been so successful if I had run for President four years ago or eight years ago, but I think that this year my candidacy coincided with a new mood in America.

After all the scandals and failures of recent years, I think our people have been looking for new voices, new ideas, a new beginning, and insofar as my campaign has been successful it is because it has been an instrument of that national desire.

This year may be the first year in our history when it is better to run for President as a peanut farmer from Plains, Georgia, than as a United States Senator from Washington, D.C.

My campaign has come a long way in the past sixteen months, from the days when they called me "Jimmy Who?"

to the recent days when they've called me the Democratic front-runner, but is still the same campaign. It has been successful because it didn't start at the top with big-name endorsements, it started at the grass roots with the support of ordinary Americans.

We went into the living rooms and union halls and we talked to the people and learned about their hopes and fears and dreams, and what we learned from thousands and thousands of people we gave back to them in a political program that reflected what they wanted, not what we wanted for them.

Our campaign has not been perfect. In retrospect, more time might have been given to this state or to that issue. Sometimes, in the heat of political combat, harsh words are spoken or overstatements made.

But overall our campaign has followed the best and surest strategy, which simply has been to take our case to the American people, to every primary in every state, and to put our faith in their good sense and good judgment.

I have never minded running in thirty primaries. If the primaries are an obstacle course, they are a necessary and wise one, for they are a test of all the qualities our people demand of their President.

Our people ask that a President be both tough and gentle, both statesman and politician, both dreamer and fighter. You expect him to have the drive and stamina to reach the White House, and the wisdom and patience to govern wisely there.

We candidates ask the people for your votes. You, in turn, ask us for our vision.

I have tried, for sixteen months, in thousands of talks across America, to express my vision of this nation's future. It is a vision that has grown and ripened as I have traveled and talked and gotten to know our people better.

Mine is a vision of an America that is, in Bob Dylan's phrase, busy being born, not busy dying.

I see an America poised not only at the brink of a new century but at the dawn of a new era of honest, compassionate, responsive government . . .

AFL-CIO Rally
Akron, Ohio
May 28, 1976

The Power of Love

In the late afternoon of June 1, after a full day of campaigning in California, Carter spoke at the dedication of a new wing of the Martin Luther King Hospital in Los Angeles. Charles Mohr, writing in the New York *Times* a few days later, described his speech as "one of the most moving speeches on the American racial dilemma heard in a long time," and noted that "An almost physical wave of love seemed to pass from the black listeners to Mr. Carter."

WE ARE here today to honor a man with a dream.

We are here to honor a man who lived and died for the cause of human brotherhood.

Martin Luther King, Jr., was the conscience of his generation.

He was a doctor to a sick society.

He was a prophet of a new and better America.

He was a Southerner, a black man, who in his too short life stood with presidents and kings and was honored around the world, but who never forgot the poor people, the oppressed people, who were his brothers and sisters and from whom he drew his strength.

He was the man, more than any other of his generation, who gazed upon the great wall of segregation and saw that it could be destroyed by the power of love.

I sometimes think that a Southerner of my generation can most fully understand the meaning and the impact of Martin Luther King's life.

He and I grew up in the same South, he the son of a clergyman, I the son of a farmer. We both knew, from opposite sides, the invisible wall of racial segregation.

The official rule then was "separate but equal," but in truth we were neither—not separate, not equal.

When I was a boy, almost all my playmates were black. We worked in the fields together, and hunted and fished and swam together, but when it was time for church or for school we went our separate ways, without really understanding why.

Our lives were dominated by unspoken, unwritten, but powerful rules, rules that were almost never challenged.

A few people challenged them, not in politics but in the way they lived their lives. My mother was one of those people. She was a nurse. She would work twelve hours a day and then come home and care for her family and minister to the people of our little community, both black and white.

My mother knew no color line. Her black friends were just as welcome in her home as her white friends, a fact that shocked some people, sometimes even my father, who was more conventional in his views on race.

I left Georgia in 1943 and went off to the Navy, and by the time I returned home ten years later the South and the nation had begun to change.

The change was slow and painful. After the Supreme Court outlawed school segregation, the wrong kind of politicians stirred up angry resistance, and little towns like mine were torn apart by fear and resentment.

Yet the change was coming. Across the South, courageous young black students demanded service at segregated lunch counters. And in the end they prevailed.

In Montgomery, a woman named Rosa Parks refused to move to the back of the bus, a young clergyman named Martin Luther King joined the protest, and a movement had found its leader.

In 1961, we had a new President, John Kennedy, who

responded to the demands of the civil rights movement, and who used the power of his office to enforce court orders at the University of Alabama and the University of Mississippi, and who by the last year of his life was giving moral leadership in the struggle for equal rights.

In August of 1963, Martin Luther King stood on the steps of the Lincoln Memorial in Washington and told a quarter of a million people of his dream for America.

"I have a dream," he said. "I have a dream that one day on the red hills of Georgia, sons of former slaves and sons of former slaveowners will be able to sit down together at the table of brotherhood.

"I have a dream," he said, "that my four little children will one day live in a nation where they will not be judged by the color of their skin but by the content of their character. I have a dream."

And so the dream was born. The challenge was made. The rest was up to America.

Three months after Dr. King's speech, President Kennedy was dead, and we had a new President, a Texan, a man whom many black people distrusted. But soon Lyndon Johnson stood before the Congress of the United States and promised, "We shall overcome!"

Lyndon Johnson carried forward the dream of equality. He used his political genius to pass the Voting Rights bill, a bill that was the best thing that happened to the South in my lifetime. The Voting Rights Act did not just guarantee the vote for black people. It liberated the South, both black and white. It made it possible for the South to come out of the past and into the mainstream of American politics.

It made it possible for a Southerner to stand before you this evening as a serious candidate for President of the United States.

But war came, and destroyed Lyndon Johnson's Great Society. Martin Luther King spoke out against that war.

There were those who told him to keep silent, who told him he would undercut his prestige if he opposed the war, but he followed his conscience and spoke his mind.

Then, in the spring of 1968, he went to Memphis to help the garbage workers get a decent wage, to help the men who did the dirtiest job for the lowest pay, and while he was there he was shot and killed.

But his dream lives on.

Perhaps some of you remember the night of Dr. King's death. Robert Kennedy was in Indianapolis, running for President, speaking before a black audience. At that point, on that awful night, Robert Kennedy was perhaps the only white politician in America who could have spoken to black people and been listened to.

Let me tell you what he said.

He said, "What we need in the United States is not division, what we need in the United States is not hatred, what we need in the United States is not violence and lawlessness, but love and wisdom and compassion toward one another, and a feeling of justice toward those who still suffer within our country, whether they be white or whether they be black."

Those words are still true today.

We lost Martin Luther King.

We lost Robert Kennedy.

We lost the election that year to men who governed without love or laughter, to men who promised law and order and gave us crime and oppression.

But the dream lived on.

It could be slowed, but never stopped.

In Atlanta, a young man named Andrew Young, who had been Martin Luther King's strong right hand, was elected to the Congress of the United States.

All over America, black men and women were carrying the dream forward into politics.

In Georgia, when I was Governor, we appointed black people to jobs and judgeships they had never held before, and one day we hung a portrait of Martin Luther King, Jr., in our State Capitol.

There were protests, but they didn't matter. Inside our State Capitol, Coretta King and Daddy King and Andy Young and I and hundreds of others joined hands and sang "We Shall Overcome."

And we shall.

I stand before you a candidate for President, a man whose life has been lifted, as yours have been, by the dream of Martin Luther King.

When I started to run for President, there were those who said I would fail, because I am from the South.

But I thought they were wrong. I thought the South was changing and America was changing. I thought the dream was taking hold.

And I ran for President throughout our nation.

We have won in the South, and we have won in the North, and now we come to the West and we ask your help.

For all our progress, we still live in a land held back by oppression and injustice.

The few who are rich and powerful still make the decisions, and the many who are poor and weak must suffer the consequences. If those in power make mistakes, it is not they or their families who lose their jobs or go on welfare or lack medical care or go to jail.

We still have poverty in the midst of plenty.

We still have far to go. We must give our government back to our people. The road will not be easy.

But we still have the dream, Martin Luther King's dream and your dream and my dream. The America we long for is still out there, somewhere ahead of us, waiting for us to find her.

I see an America poised not only at the brink of a new century but at the dawn of a new era of honest, compassionate, responsive government.

I see an American government that has turned away from

scandals and corruption and official cynicism and finally become as decent as our people.

I see an America with a tax system that does not steal from the poor and give to the rich.

I see an America with a job for every man and woman who can work, and a decent standard of living for those who cannot.

I see an America in which my child and your child and every child receives an education second to none in the world.

I see an American government that does not spy on its citizens or harass its citizens, but respects your dignity and your privacy and your right to be let alone.

I see an American foreign policy that is firm and consistent and generous, and that once again is a beacon for the hopes of the world.

I see an American President who does not govern by vetoes and negativism, but with vigor and vision and affirmative leadership, a President who is not isolated from our people but feels their pain and shares their dreams and takes his strength from them.

I see an America in which Martin Luther King's dream is our national dream.

I see an America on the move again, united, its wounds healed, its head high, a diverse and vital nation, moving into its third century with confidence and competence and compassion, an America that lives up to the majesty of its Constitution and the simple decency of its people.

This is the America that I see and that I am committed to as I run for President.

I ask your help.

You will always have mine.

Martin Luther King Hospital
Los Angeles, California
June 1, 1976

A Community of the Free

FOR THE past seventeen months, as a candidate for President, I have talked and listened to the American people.

It has been an unforgettable experience and an invaluable education. Insofar as my political campaign has been successful, it is because I have learned from our people and have accurately reflected their concerns, their frustrations, and their desires.

In the area of foreign policy, our people are troubled, confused, and sometimes angry. There has been too much emphasis on transient spectaculars and too little on substance. We are deeply concerned, not only by such obvious tragedies as the war in Vietnam, but by the more subtle erosion in the focus and the morality of our foreign policy.

Under the Nixon-Ford Administration, there has evolved a kind of secretive "Lone Ranger" foreign policy—a one-man policy of international adventure. This is not an appropriate policy for America.

We have sometimes tried to play other nations one against another instead of organizing free nations to share world responsibility in collective action. We have made highly publicized efforts to woo the major communist powers while neglecting our natural friends and allies. A foreign policy based on secrecy inherently has had to be closely guarded and amoral, and we have had to forgo openness, consultation, and a constant adherence to fundamental principles and high moral standards.

We have sought dramatic and surprising immediate results instead of long-term solutions to major problems which required careful planning in consultation with other nations.

We must be strong in our intensive resolve in order to be

strong leaders abroad. This is not possible when Congress and the American people are kept in the dark. We simply must have an international policy of democratic leadership, and we must stop trying to play a lonely game of power politics. We must evolve and consummate our foreign policy openly and frankly. There must be bipartisan harmony and collaboration between the President and the Congress, and we must re-establish a spirit of common purpose among democratic nations.

What we seek is our nation to have a foreign policy that reflects the decency and generosity and common sense of our own people.

Today I would like to speak about our alliances and the ways they can be improved to serve our national interests and the interests of others who seek peace and stability in the world.

We need to consider how, in addition to alliances that were formed in years past for essentially military purposes, we might develop broader arrangements for dealing with such problems as the arms race and world poverty and the allocation of resources.

The time has come for us to seek a partnership between North America, Western Europe, and Japan. Our three regions share economic, political, and security concerns that make it logical that we should seek ever-increasing unity and understanding.

I have traveled in Japan and Western Europe in recent years and talked to leaders there. These countries already have a significant world impact; and they are prepared to play even larger global roles in shaping a new international order.

We seek not a condominium of the powerful but a community of the free.

There are at least three areas in which the democratic nations can benefit from closer and more creative relations.

First, there are economic and political affairs. In the realm of economics, our basic purpose must be to keep open the international system in which the exchange of goods, capital, and ideas among nations can continue to expand.

Increased coordination among the industrialized democracies can help avoid the repetition of such episodes as the inflation of 1972–73 and the more recent recessions. Both were made more severe by an excess of expansionist zeal and then of deflationary reaction in North America, Japan, and Europe.

Though each country must make its own economic decisions, we need to know more about one another's interests and intentions. We must avoid unilateral acts and we must try not to work at cross-purposes in the pursuit of the same ends. We need not agree on all matters, but we should agree to discuss all matters.

There are many ways that creative alliances can work for a better world. Let me mention just one more, the area of human rights. Many of us have protested the violation of human rights in Russia, and justly so. But such violations are not limited to any one country or one ideology. There are other countries that violate human rights in one way or another—by torture, by political persecution, and by racial or religious discrimination.

We and our allies, in a creative partnership, can take the lead in establishing and promoting basic global standards of human rights. We respect the independence of all nations, but by our example, by our utterances, and by the various forms of economic and political persuasion available to us, we can quite surely lessen the injustice in this world.

We must certainly try.

Let me make one other point in the political realm. Democratic processes may in some countries bring to power parties or leaders whose ideologies are not shared by most Americans. We may not welcome these changes; we will certainly not encourage them. But we must respect the results of democratic elections and the right of countries to make their own basic ideals. We must learn to live with diversity, and we can continue to cooperate so long as such political parties respect the democratic process, uphold existing international commitments, and are not subservient to external political direction. The democratic concert of nations should exclude only those who exclude themselves by the rejection of democracy itself.

Our people have learned the folly of our trying to inject our power into the internal affairs of other nations. It is time that our government learned that lesson too.

The second area of increased cooperation among the democracies is that of mutual security. Here, however, we must recognize that the Atlantic and Pacific regions have quite different political sensitivities.

Since the United States is both an Atlantic and a Pacific power, our commitments to the security of Western Europe and of Japan are inseparable from our own security. Without these commitments, and our firm dedication to them, the political fabric of Atlantic and Pacific cooperation would be seriously weakened and world peace endangered.

As we look to the Pacific region, we see a number of changes and opportunities. Because of potential Sino-Soviet conflict, Russian and Chinese forces are not jointly deployed as our potential adversaries but confront one another along their common border. Moreover, our withdrawal from the mainland of Southeast Asia has made possible improving relationships between us and the People's Republic of China.

With regard to our primary Pacific ally, Japan, we will maintain our existing security arrangements, so long as that continues to be the wish of the Japanese people and government.

I believe it will be possible to withdraw our ground forces from South Korea on a phased basis over a time span to be determined after consultation with both South Korea and

Japan. At the same time, it should be clear to the South Korean government that its internal oppression is repugnant to our people and undermines the support for our commitment there.

We face a more immediate problem in the Atlantic sector of our defense.

The Soviet Union has in recent years strengthened its forces in Central Europe. The Warsaw Pact forces facing NATO today are substantially composed of Soviet combat troops, and these troops have been modernized and reinforced. In the event of war, they are postured for an all-out conflict of short duration and great intensity.

NATO's ground combat forces are largely European. The U. S. provides about one-fifth of the combat element, as well as the strategic umbrella, and without this American commitment Western Europe could not defend itself successfully.

In recent years, new military technology has been developed by both sides, including precision-guided munitions that are changing the nature of land warfare.

Unfortunately, NATO's arsenal suffers from a lack of standardization, which needlessly increases the cost of NATO, and its strategy too often seems wedded to past plans and concepts. We must not allow our alliance to become an anachronism.

There is, in short, a pressing need for us and our allies to undertake a review of NATO's forces and its strategies in light of the changing military environment.

Even as we review our military posture, we must spare no effort to bring about a reduction of the forces that confront one another in Central Europe.

It is to be hoped that the stalemated force-reduction talks in Vienna will soon produce results so that the forces of both sides can be reduced in a manner that impairs the security of neither. The requirement of balanced reductions complicates negotiations, but it is an important requirement for the maintenance of security in Europe.

Similarly, in the SALT talks we must seek significant nuclear disarmament that safeguards the basic interests of both sides.

Let me say something I have often said in recent months. East-West relations will be both cooperative and competitive for a long time to come. We want the competition to be peaceful, and we want the cooperation to increase. But we will never seek accommodation at the expense of our own national interests or the interests of our allies.

Our potential adversaries are intelligent people. They respect strength, they respect constancy, they respect candor. They will understand our commitment to our allies. They will listen even more carefully if we and our allies speak with a common resolve.

We must remember too that a genuine spirit of cooperation between the democracies and the Soviet Union should extend beyond a negative cessation of hostilities and reach toward joint efforts in dealing with such world problems as agricultural development and the population crisis.

The great challenge we Americans confront is to demonstrate to the Soviet Union that our good will is as great as our strength until, despite all the obstacles, our two nations can achieve new attitudes and new trust, and until in time the terrible burden of the arms race can be lifted from our people.

One realistic step would be to recognize that thus far, while we have had certain progress on a bilateral basis, we have continued to confront each other by proxy in various trouble spots. These indirect challenges may be potentially more dangerous than face-to-face disagreements, and at best they make mockery of the very concept of détente. If we want genuine progress, it must be at every level.

Our democracies must also work together more closely in a joint effort to help the hundreds of millions of people on this planet who are living in poverty and despair.

We have all seen the growth of North-South tensions in world affairs, tensions that are often based on legitimate economic grievances. We have seen in the Middle East the juncture of East-West and North-South conflicts and the resultant threat to world peace.

The democratic nations must respond to the challenge of human need on three levels.

First, by widening the opportunities for genuine North-South consultations.

Secondly, by assisting those nations that are in direst need.

There are many ways the democracies can unite to help shape a more stable and just world order. We can work to lower trade barriers and make a major effort to provide increased support to the international agencies that now make capital available to the Third World.

Third, we and our allies must work together to limit the flow of arms into the developing world.

The North-South conflict is in part a security problem. As long as the more powerful nations exploit the less powerful, they will be repaid by terrorism, hatred, and potential violence. Insofar as our policies are selfish or cynical or shortsighted, there will inevitably be a day of reckoning.

I am particularly concerned by our nation's role as the world's leading arms salesman. We sold or gave away billions of dollars of arms last year, mostly to developing nations. . . . Sometimes we try to justify this unsavory business on the cynical ground that by rationing out the means of violence we can somehow control the world's violence.

The fact is that we cannot have it both ways. Can we be both the world's leading champion of peace and the world's leading supplier of the weapons of war? If I become President I will work with our allies, some of whom are selling arms, and also seek to work with the Soviets, to increase the emphasis on peace and to reduce the commerce in weapons of war.

The challenge we and our allies face with regard to the

developing nations is a great one, a constant one, and an exciting one. It is exciting because it calls for so much creativity at so many levels by so many nations and individuals.

I have suggested steps which we and our allies might take toward a more stable and more just world order. I do not pretend to have all the answers. I hope you will help me find them.

What I do have is a strong sense that this country is drifting and must have new leadership and new direction. The time has come for a new thrust of creativity in foreign policy equal to that of the years following the Second World War. The old international institutions no longer suffice. The time has come for a new architectural effort, with creative initiative by our own nation, with growing cooperation among the industrial democracies its cornerstone, and with peace and justice its constant goal.

The Foreign Policy Association
New York, New York
June 23, 1976

3

Toward
the
Presidency

July–November 1976

My Name Is Jimmy Carter and
I'm Running for President

MY NAME is Jimmy Carter, and I'm running for President. It's been a long time since I said those words the first time, and now I've come here after seeing our great country to accept your nomination.

I accept it, in the words of John F. Kennedy, with a full and grateful heart and with only one obligation: to devote every effort of body, mind, and spirit to lead our party back to victory and our nation back to greatness.

It's a pleasure to be here with all you Democrats and to see that our Bicentennial celebration and our Bicentennial convention has been one of decorum and order without any fights or free-for-alls. Among Democrats that can only happen once every two hundred years. With this kind of a united Democratic Party, we are ready, and eager, to take on the Republicans—whichever Republican Party they decide to send against us in November.

Nineteen seventy-six will not be a year of politics as usual. It can be a year of inspiration and hope, and it will be a year of concern, of quiet and sober reassessment of our nation's character and purpose. It has already been a year when voters have confounded the experts. And I guarantee you that it will be the year when we give the government of this country back to the people of this country.

There is a new mood in America. We have been shaken by a tragic war abroad and by scandals and broken promises at home. Our people are searching for new voices and new ideas and new leaders.

Although government has its limits and cannot solve all our problems, we Americans reject the view that we must be reconciled to failures and mediocrity, or to an inferior quality of life. For I believe that we can come through this time of trouble stronger than ever. Like troops who have been in combat, we have been tempered in the fire; we have been disciplined, and we have been educated. Guided by lasting and simple moral values, we have emerged idealists without illusions, realists who still know the old dreams of justice and liberty, of country and of community.

This year we have had thirty state primaries—more than ever before—making it possible to take our campaign directly to the people of America: to homes and shopping centers, to factory shift lines and colleges, to beauty parlors and barbershops, to farmers' markets and union halls.

This has been a long and personal campaign—a humbling experience, reminding us that ultimate political influence rests not with the power brokers but with the people. This has been a time for learning and for the exchange of ideas, a time of tough debate on the important issues facing our country. This kind of debate is part of our tradition, and as Democrats we are heirs to a great tradition.

I have never met a Democratic President, but I have always been a Democrat.

Years ago, as a farm boy sitting outdoors with my family on the ground in the middle of the night, gathered close around a battery radio connected to the automobile battery and listening to the Democratic conventions in far-off cities, I was a long way from the selection process. I feel much closer to it tonight.

Ours is the party of the man who was nominated by those distant conventions and who inspired and restored this nation in its darkest hours—Franklin D. Roosevelt.

Ours is the party of a fighting Democrat who showed us that a common man could be an uncommon leader—Harry S. Truman.

Ours is the party of a brave young President who called

the young at heart, regardless of age, to seek a "New Frontier" of national greatness—John F. Kennedy.

And ours is also the party of a great-hearted Texan who took office in a tragic hour and who went on to do more than any other President in this century to advance the cause of human rights—Lyndon Johnson.

Our party was built out of the sweatshops of the old Lower East Side, the dark mills of New Hampshire, the blazing hearths of Illinois, the coal mines of Pennsylvania, the hardscrabble farms of the southern coastal plains, and the unlimited frontiers of America.

Ours is the party that welcomed generations of immigrants —the Jews, the Irish, the Italians, the Poles, and all the others, enlisted them in its ranks and fought the political battles that helped bring them into the American mainstream. And they have shaped the character of our party.

That is our heritage. Our party has not been perfect. We have made mistakes, and we have paid for them. But ours is a tradition of leadership and compassion and progress.

Our leaders have fought for every piece of progressive legislation, from RFD and REA to Social Security and civil rights. In times of need, the Democrats were there.

But in recent years our nation has seen a failure of leadership. We have been hurt, and we have been disillusioned. We have seen a wall go up that separates us from our own government.

We have lost some precious things that historically have bound our people and our government together. We feel that moral decay has weakened our country, that it is crippled by a lack of goals and values, and that our public officials have lost faith in us.

We have been a nation adrift too long. We have been without leadership too long. We have had divided and deadlocked government too long. We have been governed by veto too long. We have suffered enough at the hands of a tired and worn-out administration without new ideas, without youth or vitality, without vision and without the confidence of the American people. There is a fear that our best years are behind us. But I say to you that our nation's best is still ahead.

Our country has lived through a time of torment. It is now a time for healing. We want to have faith again. We want to be proud again. We just want the truth again.

It is time for the people to run the government, and not the other way around.

It is the time to honor and strengthen our families and our neighborhoods and our diverse cultures and customs.

We need a Democratic President and a Congress to work in harmony for a change, with mutual respect for a change. And next year we are going to have that new leadership. You can depend on it!

It is time for America to move and to speak not with boasting and belligerence but with a quiet strength, to depend in world affairs not merely on the size of an arsenal but on the nobility of ideas, and to govern at home not by confusion and crisis but with grace and imagination and common sense.

Too many have had to suffer at the hands of a political and economic elite who have shaped decisions and never had to account for mistakes or to suffer from injustice. When unemployment prevails, they never stand in line looking for a job. When deprivation results from a confused and bewildering welfare system, they never do without food or clothing or a place to sleep. When the public schools are inferior or torn by strife, their children go to exclusive private schools. And when the bureaucracy is bloated and confused, the powerful always manage to discover and occupy niches of special influence and privilege. An unfair tax structure serves their needs. And tight secrecy always seems to prevent reform.

All of us must be careful not to cheat each other. Too often unholy, self-perpetuating alliances have been formed between money and politics, and the average citizen has been held at arm's length.

Each time our nation has made a serious mistake the American people have been excluded from the process. The tragedy of Vietnam and Cambodia, the disgrace of Watergate, and the embarrassment of the CIA revelations could have been avoided if our government had simply reflected the sound judgment and good common sense and the high moral character of the American people.

It is time for us to take a new look at our own government, to strip away the secrecy, to expose the unwarranted pressure of lobbyists, to eliminate waste, to release our civil servants from bureaucratic chaos, to provide tough management, and always to remember that in any town or city the mayor, the governor, and the President represent exactly the same constituents.

As a governor, I had to deal each day with the complicated and confused and overlapping and wasteful federal government bureaucracy. As President, I want you to help me evolve an efficient, economical, purposeful, and manageable government for our nation. Now, I recognize the difficulty, but if I'm elected, it's going to be done. And you can depend on it!

We must strengthen the government closest to the people. Business, labor, agriculture, education, science, and government should not struggle in isolation from one another but should be able to strive toward mutual goals and shared opportunities. We should make major investments in people and not in buildings and weapons. The poor, the aged, the weak, the afflicted must be treated with respect and compassion and with love.

I have spoken a lot of times this year about love. But love must be aggressively translated into simple justice. The test of any government is not how popular it is with the powerful but how honestly and fairly it deals with those who must depend on it.

It is time for a complete overhaul of our income tax system. I still tell you: It is a disgrace to the human race. All my life I have heard promises about tax reform, but it never quite happens. With your help, we are finally going to make it happen. And you can depend on it.

Here is something that can really help our country: It is time for universal voter registration.

It is time for a nationwide comprehensive health program for all our people.

It is time to guarantee an end to discrimination because of race or sex by full involvement in the decision-making processes of government by those who know what it is to suffer from discrimination. And they'll be in the government if I am elected.

It is time for the law to be enforced. We cannot educate children, we cannot create harmony among our people, we cannot preserve basic human freedom unless we have an orderly society.

Crime and lack of justice are especially cruel to those who are least able to protect themselves. Swift arrest and trial, fair and uniform punishment, should be expected by anyone who would break our laws.

It is time for our government leaders to respect the law no less than the humblest citizen, so that we can end once and for all a double standard of justice. I see no reason why big-shot crooks should go free and the poor ones go to jail.

A simple and a proper function of government is just to make it easy for us to do good and difficult for us to do wrong.

As an engineer, a planner, a businessman, I see clearly the value to our nation of a strong system of free enterprise based on increased productivity and adequate wages. We Democrats believe that competition is better than regulation, and we intend to combine strong safeguards for consumers with minimal intrusion of government in our free economic system.

I believe that anyone who is able to work ought to work—and ought to have a chance to work. We will never have an end to the inflationary spiral, we will never have a balanced budget—which I am determined to see—as long as we have eight or nine million Americans out of work who cannot find a job. Any system of economics is bankrupt if it sees either value or virtue in unemployment. We simply cannot check inflation by keeping people out of work.

The foremost responsibility of any President, above all else, is to guarantee the security of our nation—a guarantee of freedom from the threat of successful attack or blackmail, and the ability with our allies to maintain peace.

But peace is not the mere absence of war. Peace is action to stamp out international terrorism. Peace is the unceasing effort to preserve human rights. Peace is a combined demonstration of strength and good will. We will pray for peace and we will work for peace, until we have removed from all nations for all time the threat of nuclear destruction.

America's birth opened a new chapter in mankind's history. Ours was the first nation to dedicate itself clearly to basic moral and philosophical principles: that all people are created equal and endowed with inalienable rights to life, liberty, and the pursuit of happiness, and that the power of government is derived from the consent of the governed.

This national commitment was a singular act of wisdom and courage, and it brought the best and the bravest from other nations to our shores. It was a revolutionary development that captured the imagination of mankind. It created a basis for a unique role for America—that of a pioneer in shaping more decent and just relations among people and among societies.

Today, two hundred years later, we must address ourselves to that role, both in what we do at home and how we act abroad—among people everywhere who have become politically more alert, socially more congested, and increasingly impatient with global inequities, and who are now organized, as you know, into some one hundred and fifty different nations. This calls for nothing less than a sustained architectural effort to shape an international framework of peace within which our own ideals gradually can become a global reality.

Our nation should always derive its character directly from the people and let this be the strength and the image to be presented to the world—the character of the American people.

To our friends and allies I say that what unites us through our common dedication to democracy is much more important than that which occasionally divides us on economics or politics. To the nations that seek to lift themselves from poverty I say that America shares your aspirations and extends its hand to you. To those nation-states that wish to compete with us I say that we neither fear competition nor see it as an obstacle to wider cooperation. To all people I say that after two hundred years America still remains confident and youthful in its commitment to freedom and equality, and we always will be.

During this election year we candidates will ask you for your votes, and from us will be demanded our vision.

My vision of this nation and its future has been deepened and matured during the nineteen months that I have campaigned among you for President. I have never had more faith in America than I do today. We have an America that, in Bob Dylan's phrase, is busy being born, not busy dying.

We can have an America that has reconciled its economic needs with its desire for an environment that we can pass on with pride to the next generation.

We can have an America that provides excellence in education to my child and your child and every child.

We can have an America that encourages and takes pride in our ethnic diversity, our religious diversity, our cultural diversity—knowing that out of this pluralistic heritage has come the strength and the vitality and the creativity that has made us great and will keep us great.

We can have an American government that does not oppress or spy on its own people but respects our dignity and our privacy and our right to be let alone.

We can have an America where freedom, on the one hand, and equality, on the other hand, are mutually supportive and not in conflict, and where the dreams of our nation's first leaders are fully realized in our own day and age.

And we can have an America which harnesses the idealism of the student, the compassion of a nurse or the social worker, the determination of a farmer, the wisdom of a teacher, the practicality of the business leader, the experience of the senior citizen, and the hope of a laborer to build a better life for us all. And we can have it, and we're going to have it!

As I've said many times before, we can have an American President who does not govern with negativism and fear of the future, but with vigor and vision and aggressive leadership—a President who's not isolated from the people, but who feels your pain and shares your dreams and takes his strength and his wisdom and his courage from you.

I see an America on the move again, united, a diverse and vital and tolerant nation, entering our third century with pride and confidence, an America that lives up to the majesty of our Constitution and the simple decency of our people.

This is the America we want. This is the America that we will have.

We will go forward from this convention with some differences of opinion perhaps, but nevertheless united in a calm determination to make our country large and driving and generous in spirit once again, ready to embark on great national deeds. And once again, as brothers and sisters, our hearts will swell with pride to call ourselves Americans.

Acceptance Speech
Democratic National Convention
New York, New York
July 15, 1976

A Special Responsibility

Warren Beatty was the host for a reception for Carter at the Beverly Wilshire Hotel that was attended by about fifty movie and television personalities, including Carroll O'Connor, Louise Lasser, Sidney Poitier, Faye Dunaway, Paul Simon, Diana Ross, Robert Altman, James Caan, and George Peppard. A question-and-answer session was spirited and often light-hearted. At one point, actor Tony Randall asked Carter if he would support a national opera or national theater. Carter said he had never been asked that question before. "You've never met with people of this level," Randall said. "That's why I'm the nominee," Carter replied. But near the end of his remarks, Carter turned serious and spoke of the obligation more fortunate members of society have to the less fortunate. His remarks were taped by Los Angeles *Times* reporter Kenneth Reich, who was present as a pool reporter.

... IF WE make a mistake, the chances are we won't actually go to prison, and if we don't like the public school system, we put our kids in private schools. But the overwhelming majority of the American people are touched directly and personally when government is ill-managed or insensitive or callous or unconcerned about those kinds of problems.

When the tax structure is modified, which Congress does almost every year, you can rest assured that powerful people who are well organized, who have good lawyers, who have lobbyists in Washington, don't get cheated. But there are millions of people in this country who do get cheated, and they are the very ones who can't afford it. So there are a multitude of needs.

We take transportation for granted. We can go out and get in our Chevrolet or our Buick or our Cadillac or our Rolls-Royce and go anywhere we want to. A lot of people don't have automobiles. I can go a mile from my house, I can go two hundred yards from my house, and people are there who are very poor, and when they get sick it's almost impossible for them to get a doctor.

In the county where I farm, we don't have a doctor, we don't have a dentist, we don't have a pharmacist, we don't have a registered nurse; and people who live there who are very poor have no access to health care. We found in Georgia through a three-year study that poor women, who are mostly black, in rural areas have twenty times more cervical cancer than white women in urban counties, just because they haven't seen a doctor, because the disease has gone so far that it can't be corrected.

There's a need for public officials—Presidents, governors, congressmen and others—to bypass the lobbyists and the special-interest groups and our own circle of friends who are very fortunate, and try to understand those who are dependent on government to give them a decent life. That is what I hope to do.

When people organize, there's an almost built-in separation from the kind of people I've just been describing. Doctors really care about their patients, but when doctors organize and hire a lobbyist, the lobbyist doesn't give a damn about the patients.

Schoolteachers love their students. They quite often serve at a sacrificial salary compared to what they should get, but when they organize and hire a lobbyist to work with the Legislature, those lobbyists don't care anything about students.

The same with lawyers. They really take care of their clients, but when those lawyers organize and get a lobbyist, those lobbyists don't care anything about clients. The same thing with farmers and with people in business.

So I say public servants, like me and Jerry Brown and others, have a special responsibility to bypass the big shots, including you and people like you, and like I was, and to make a concerted effort to understand people who are poor, black, speak a foreign language, who are not well educated, who are inarticulate, who are timid, who have some monumental problem, and at the same time to run the government in a competent way—well-organized, efficient, manageable— so that those services which are so badly needed can be delivered.

Reception
Los Angeles, California
August 2, 1976

We Have Been Through Too Much in Too Short a Time

DURING THE past week, when the attention of the political world was focused on the events in Kansas City, I spent most of my time at my home in Plains, Georgia, reading, studying national issues, talking with friends and advisers, and trying to sort out my thoughts as I look ahead to the Presidential campaign.

I want to share some of those thoughts with you today, and I want to say at the outset that my mood is one of confidence and optimism. Not simply optimism over my own immediate political prospects, but optimism about the future of this country.

I think, and I believe the American people agree, that this is one of our most important elections, that this is one of those elections, as in 1932 and 1960, when we have a chance to break with the past and make a fresh start in our national affairs.

Every election is unique, of course. In 1932 our nation faced an economic disaster, and our people correctly judged that Franklin Roosevelt was the candidate whose personal character and political courage made him best qualified to lead us through that crisis.

In 1960 we faced not an economic crisis but a state of spiritual malaise, a sense of national drift, and the people correctly judged that John Kennedy, with all his youth and vigor, could keep his promise to get the country moving again, as in fact he did.

Today, as we face the election of 1976, I think there is a feeling in the land, much like those of 1932 and 1960, that we face an economic crisis and that we are drifting and need to get moving again. But there is something more than that. After all we have been through in recent years, we need to have our faith in our government restored. We want to believe once again that our national leaders are honorable and competent and deserving of our trust. For if we cannot believe that, little else matters.

I have thought for some time that this year's campaign was taking place on two distinct levels. At one level, and quite properly, there is policy and the economy. In many hundreds of public forums I have discussed all these issues with our people for twenty months, and later this month I will make statements on defense and veterans' affairs, agriculture and economics. But today I would like to discuss with you the other level of this year's campaign, the less tangible issue, which is simply the desire of the American people to have faith again in our own government.

We have been through too much in too short a time. Our national nightmare began with the assassination of John Kennedy, and went on to include the assassination of Robert Kennedy, and of Martin Luther King, Jr., and the wounding of George Wallace. We watched the widespread opposition to the war in Vietnam, and the division and bitterness that war caused, and the violence in Chicago in 1968, and the invasion of Cambodia, and the shootings at Kent State, and revelations of official lying and spying and bugging, the resignations in disgrace of both a President and a Vice President, and the disclosure that our top security and law enforcement agencies were deliberately and routinely violating the law.

No other generation in American history has ever been subjected to such a battering as this. Small wonder then that the politics of 1976 have turned out to be significantly different from years past. I doubt that four years ago or eight years ago a former Southern governor with no national reputation and no Washington experience would have been able to win the Democratic nomination for President. But this year many voters were looking for new leaders, leaders who were not associated with the mistakes of the past.

This is suggested not only by my own campaign but by the success that Governor Jerry Brown achieved in several of the Democratic primaries, and that Governor Reagan achieved in the Republican campaign. For, however else we may differ, Governors Brown and Reagan and I have in common the fact that we are all outsiders as far as Washington is concerned, and committed to major changes in our nation's government if elected President.

To want a change, to want a fresh start, to want government that is honest and competent again, is not a partisan issue. Democrats and Republicans, liberals and conservatives, all share those fundamental concerns.

In the last analysis, good government is not a matter of being liberal or conservative. Good government is the art of doing what is right, and that is far more difficult. To be liberal or conservative requires only ideology; to do what is right requires sensitivity and wisdom.

I think that most Americans are not very ideological. Most Americans share a deep-seated desire for two goals that might, to an ideological person, seem contradictory. We want both progress and preservation.

We want progress because progress is the very essence of our American dream—the belief that each generation, through hard work, can give a better life to its children. And increasingly in this century we have realized that it is a proper function of government to help make that dream come true.

But we do not want reckless change. We want to preserve what is best in our past—our political traditions, our cultural heritage, our physical resources—as guideposts to our future.

To walk the line between progress and preservation, between too much change and too little, is no easy task. It cannot be achieved by the extremists of either side, by those who scorn the past or those who fear the future. It can only be accomplished by leaders who are independent and imaginative and flexible in their thinking, and are guided not by closed minds but by common sense.

That is the kind of leadership the American people are looking for this year, and that is the kind of leadership that, if elected, I intend to provide.

As I have observed the political world in recent years, it has seemed to me that there is a process at work, in both political parties and probably in all nations, by which over a period of time the political leadership becomes isolated from, and different from, the people they are supposed to serve.

It seems almost inevitable that if political leaders stay in power too long . . . and eat expensive meals in private clubs too long, they are going to become cut off from the lives and concerns of ordinary Americans. It is almost like a law of nature. As Lord Acton said, power tends to corrupt.

I think this process reached a peak a few years ago, when we had a President who surrounded himself with people who knew everything in the world about merchandising and manipulation and winning elections, and nothing at all about the hopes and fears and dreams of average people.

When government becomes cut off from its people, when its leaders are talking only to themselves instead of addressing reality, then it is time for a process of national self-renewal, time to look outside the existing governing class for new leaders with new ideas. I think that is what happened in the Democratic Party this year. I think our party was ready for renewal, for new faces, for a changing of the guard. If the candidate had not been myself, I think we would have chosen someone else who was not part of the old order of things.

My sense is that millions of Americans feel that this is the year in which they will give the system one last chance. They do not want to be disillusioned again. They are going to study the candidates, examine our political records and our personal ability and character, and make a judgment as to which candidate can best restore competence and vision and honesty to our government.

I welcome their scrutiny, and have confidence in their judgment.

I think the basic issue in this campaign is going to be whether we want government that looks confidently to the future, or government that clings fearfully to the past.

There's a song in the musical *Oklahoma* called "Everything's Up to Date in Kansas City." But I don't think everything was up to date in Kansas City last week. We kept hearing the same old tired rhetoric about socialism and reckless spending. I don't think the American people are much impressed by that kind of rhetoric. The American people don't believe that Social Security and Medicare were reckless spending, or that TVA and the minimum wage were socialism. The American people consider the source of those charges and look at the record and aren't deceived by the nay-sayers.

One of the real issues in this campaign is going to be President Ford's record of vetoes. It is a record that I cite more in sorrow than in anger, for it is a record of political insensitivity, of missed opportunities, of constant conflict with the Congress, and of national neglect.

In six years as President, Mr. Ford's predecessor vetoed forty-one bills that had been passed by Congress. In only two years, Ford has already vetoed fifty-three bills, about four times as many bills per year as his predecessor—and to be four times as negative as Mr. Ford's predecessor is a remarkable achievement.

What did these vetoes accomplish? Did they save us from wasteful, reckless spending, as the administration would like us to believe? I think not.

One of the bills President Ford vetoed was the Emergency Employment Act, which would have created nearly two million full and part-time jobs to help those millions of Americans who have been rendered jobless by Republican economic policies. I think our government has a responsibility to help those people get back to work. When people can't find jobs, we pay the price over and over in increased costs of welfare and unemployment compensation and lost tax revenues.

Congress also passed a bill that would have granted those unemployed homeowners temporary help in meeting their mortgage payments. I think that was a responsible action for Congress to take. But Mr. Ford vetoed the bill.

When people are out of work, they and their children still have to eat, and Congress passed the School Lunch Act, to increase the number of families whose children were eligible for school lunch subsidies. But Mr. Ford vetoed that bill.

I had occasion, very close to home, to see what that kind of veto could mean to the real people who were on the receiving end of it. I know a young teacher who taught a remedial class for first-graders in the Plains Elementary School. Most of the students in this special class happened to be black, and were having a hard time getting started in school because of the devastating poverty in which they had been raised.

Free milk was provided twice a day, in the morning and at lunch, for needy students, but then there was a cutback and the morning milk was eliminated. So the young teacher began using her own money to see that all her students had milk. And when she ran out of money she went to her father and he saw to it that her students had milk every morning.

That is the sort of thing that happens when our leaders ignore the human factor in government, when they think in terms of statistics and economic theories instead of in terms of real human needs.

These leaders are so short-sighted. Doesn't it make more

sense to spend money on milk and education today, to help children get a fair start in life, than to spend money on police and courts and jails ten years from now, when those children have grown up untrained for a productive life and turned against a society that treated their needs with indifference?

It has been my experience in government that the most profitable investment is in people, and that is the rule I will follow if I become your President.

There were many other vetoes. Mr. Ford vetoed a bill to provide loans and grants to train nurses. He vetoed a bill to send more doctors to rural areas and inner-city slums where there are far too few doctors. He vetoed a bill to provide job training and college educations for Vietnam veterans, the most unappreciated heroes in our nation's history.

These vetoes haven't helped our economy. They haven't balanced the budget—far from it. They have only contributed to needless human suffering.

An occasional veto may be justified, if legislation is poorly drafted or ill-considered, but fifty-three vetoes in two years demonstrates a negativism, a dormancy, and a fear of action that can only be harmful to this country. There is something seriously wrong when the members of Congress, all of whom were elected by the people, repeatedly pass legislation the country needs, only to have it vetoed by an appointed President. I believe those men and women in Congress are a great deal closer to the national mood than Mr. Ford has shown himself to be.

We have had enough of government by veto. It is time we had a President who will lead our nation, and who will work in harmony with Congress for a change, with mutual respect for a change, out in the open for a change, so the working families of this country can be represented as well as the rich and the powerful and the special-interest groups.

Another major issue this fall is going to be the state of our nation's economy. Republicans have a long tradition of mishandling the economy, one that goes back to Herbert Hoover.

Except in election years, when they sometimes manage to make the economy pick up by temporarily adopting Democratic economic programs.

During the Eisenhower, Nixon, and Ford administrations, we had five recessions. Under Kennedy and Johnson we had none. And we all know that recessions are hardest on those people who are weakest, who are poor and uneducated and isolated, who are confused and inarticulate, who are often unemployed and chronically dependent—in short, those members of society whom a good government would be trying hardest to help.

Do you know what the basic Republican anti-inflation policy has been? To put people out of work. Cooling down the economy, they call it, because that sounds nicer. I say to you that any economic policy that sees virtue in unemployment is morally and politically and intellectually bankrupt.

What's more, those policies have been dismal failures. In 1968, the last year of a Democratic Administration, the unemployment rate was 3.6 percent. Today it's more than twice that—about 7.8 percent and rising. Under Kennedy and Johnson the average annual rate of inflation was 2 percent. During the Nixon and Ford administrations it has been almost 7 percent.

With all this human suffering, has the Republican Administration balanced the budget? In the last three years, the accumulated deficits are about a hundred and sixty billion dollars, more than the previous thirty years combined. Under Kennedy and Johnson, the average deficit was less than four billion dollars. Under Nixon and Ford the average deficit has been more than twenty-four billion dollars a year.

In short, the Republican economic policies have not worked, and I believe they have failed to work because they were the creations of people who put economic theories and special interests ahead of the realities of human need in this country.

There are many other problems and many other issues in

this campaign. I have been speaking about the breakdown of the American family, and I mentioned that among young people the second most prevalent cause of death is suicide and that in the past ten years the gonorrhea rate has tripled among children fourteen years of age or younger.

I sensed that some people thought I shouldn't use those words "suicide" and "gonorrhea" because they are ugly words describing unpleasant facts. But there are many unpleasant problems in our society—children who need food, overcrowded jails and mental institutions, inadequate treatment for the young men who were maimed in Vietnam, and the heartbreak and family disintegration that unemployment can bring.

All these are ugly problems and it is a natural human instinct for us to want to tune them out. But we cannot tune them out. We can only succeed in tuning out our own humanity, including those qualities of compassion and concern without which no society, however rich or powerful, can be truly great.

"No man is an island," John Donne wrote many years ago; we are all part of the mainland of humanity. That is still true today; and as American citizens, most of us are blessed with a good education and influence in society. We cannot ignore the needs and suffering of our less fortunate fellow citizens— not if we want this nation to remain great.

The Town Hall Forum
Los Angeles, California
August 23, 1976

Pardon Yes, Amnesty No

Carter knew that his pledge to grant pardons by Vietnam draft evaders would meet with disapproval by many members of the American Legion. But as he prepared his remarks for the Legion's annual convention, he told an aide that he intended to "meet the issue head-on." The body of his speech was well received—interrupted by perhaps twenty bursts of applause. But when Carter declared his intention to grant pardons for draft evaders, he was interrupted by about forty-five seconds of boos and cries of "No." Then Carter continued with his speech and was cheered several times more as he made additional points with which the Legionnaires agreed.

MR. COMMANDER and my fellow Legionnaires. I'm very, very proud to be here this morning to meet with all of you and to spend a few minutes together thinking about our country.

I am, as you may know, a member of Legion Post Number Two, in Americus, Georgia, as was my father before me. A tradition of military service runs deep in my family, as in many of yours. My first ancestor to live in Georgia, whose name was also James Carter, fought in the Revolutionary War. Almost a hundred years later other members of my family fought in the War between the States; and my father, Earl Carter, served as a first lieutenant in the Army during the First World War. I spent eleven years in the Navy, most of my sea duty in submarines. I had the good fortune to serve under Admiral Hyman Rickover on the development of the second atomic submarine.

My oldest son, Jack, continued our family's tradition in

the military. But his service came in a different era, quite different from my own. Jack left college and volunteered to serve in the armed forces. He did so because he didn't think it was right for him to avoid the draft simply because he had the money and the educational background to stay in college. So he went to Vietnam.

During the Second World War, even during the Korean War, I always wore my uniform with immense pride, and it was a badge of honor not only in the military but among my civilian friends and neighbors as well. But that was not the case when my son Jack came back from Da Nang in 1969.

He and the uniform he wore were all too often greeted with scorn and jokes. Many of his friends told him he was a fool to risk his life in a meaningless war that couldn't be won. Hundreds of thousands of Vietnam veterans were meeting the same bitter reception all over America. I believe we should love our country and be proud of our country and willing to fight to defend our country. That's how you and I grew up, never doubting that ours was the greatest nation on earth.

But we must recognize that for many of our fellow Americans patriotism is out of fashion. That fact is part of the bitter heritage of an unpopular war.

I don't seek a blind or an uncritical patriotism. Obviously, a government's policy must be deserving of public support. But in recent years disagreement with our nation's policies often became rejection of our nation itself and what it stands for. There's a great need for the next President to do everything in his power by word and deed to restore national pride and patriotism in our country, and if I'm elected that's what I intend to do.

I did not come here today just to get your vote or your endorsement or just to make a good impression on you. I come here as a nominee for President—with a likely prospect of being elected, not a sure thing—who spent full time the last

twenty months learning about this country, what it is and
what it ought to be.

I want to talk to you about some tough decisions—as veterans of course, but also as Americans who are farmers and
truck drivers and doctors and lawyers and fathers and grand-
fathers and schoolteachers and civil servants, employed, unemployed, rich, poor—just between us as Americans.

The first thing I want to say is we must maintain adequate
military strength compared to that of our potential adversaries. This relative strength can only be assured by a national
commitment to necessary military expenditures, by the elimination of waste, duplication among forces, excessive personnel costs, unnecessary new weapons systems, inefficient
contracting procedures, and by a constant search for peace,
so that armament levels over a period of time can be reduced
among all nations.

The most important single factor in avoiding nuclear war
is a mutual desire for peace that exists among the superpowers of the world. I would never again see our nation
become militarily involved in the internal affairs of another
country unless our own security is directly threatened.

But it is absolutely imperative that the world know that
we will meet obligations and commitments to our allies and
that we will always keep our nation strong. We must also
remember that excessive foreign commitments can overtax
our national ability. We must therefore be cautious in making
commitments, but firm in honoring commitments that we've
made.

As we seek an adequate defense, we must face the fact
that the very words "national security" have fallen into dis-
repute. I want to hear those words spoken with respect once
again. Too often those words are now suspect because they
have been misused by political leaders to hide a multitude
of sins, and because they have been used to justify inefficiency and waste in the Pentagon. Whatever the price and

whatever the pressures, the President must insist on armed forces that are lean and muscular and flexible, not a confused bureaucracy but a tough fighting force. That's what we need; that's what we must maintain.

We must always recognize that the best way to meet ideological threats around the world is to make our own democratic system work right here at home. The strongest defense grows out of a strong homefront. Our defense must come not only from fighting forces but from our people's trust in our own leaders. From adequate transportation, energy, agriculture, science, education, employment, and most of all from the willingness of our people, when necessary, to make a personal sacrifice for the sake of our nation. Not until we restore national unity can we have a truly adequate national defense. Only then, in Theodore Roosevelt's phrase, can we "speak softly but carry a big stick."

In our country we must recognize that in far too many cases the Vietnam veteran in particular has been a victim of governmental insensitivity and neglect. Large bureaucracies have often been incompetent, inefficient, and unresponsive to their responsibility to veterans. Each month thousands of veterans are plagued with late delivery of badly needed benefit checks. Hundreds of millions of dollars in benefit payments have been improperly computed. The average VA hospital has only half the doctors and supporting personnel found in the average community hospital for civilians.

The poor record of the government bureaucracy has been especially bad in programs intended to help recent veterans to find jobs.

Last month there were still 543,000 Vietnam veterans who had no jobs. The reason for this dismal record is clear. It's a failure of leadership.

I believe we need to address the needs of veterans, especially the Vietnam veterans, with sympathetic and active leadership rather than with vetoes and with passive resistance. Men and women who have endured so much suffering, so bravely, fighting in a far-off land should not now suffer anew in their own country at the hands of insensitive bureaucrats and indifferent politicians. That's got to be changed, and I intend to do it.

If I become President, the American veteran, of all ages, of all wars, is going to have a friend and a comrade and a firm ally in the White House.

Now I would like to speak for a moment about the issue of amnesty. Where I come from most of the men who went off to fight in Vietnam were poor. They did not want to move to Canada. They didn't know where Sweden was. They didn't have the money to hide from the draft in college. Many of them thought it was a bad war, but they went anyway. A lot of them came back with scarred minds and bodies or with missing limbs. Some fifty thousand didn't come back at all. They suffered under the threat of death. And they still suffer from the indifference of many of their fellow Americans. The Vietnam veterans are our nation's greatest unsung heroes.

In my own mind I could never equate what they have done with what those who left this country did to avoid the draft. But I think it's time for the damage and the hatred and the divisiveness of the Vietnam war to be over.

I do not favor—and I want you to listen carefully because I don't want you to misunderstand me—I do not favor a blanket amnesty; but for those who violated Selective Service laws I intend to grant a blanket pardon.

To me there's a difference. Amnesty means that what you did was right; a pardon means that what you did, right or wrong, is forgiven. So a pardon yes, amnesty no. For deserters each case should be handled on an individual basis in accordance with our nation's system of military justice.

Now I realize, I realized before I made my statement to you, that everybody would not agree. I'm a veteran myself, a member of the American Legion. But I want to spell out my position to you because of this: Our nation is still divided. There's still a lot of hatred, there's still a lot of division, there's still an absence of support for our military personnel left over from the Vietnamese war. I think it's time to get that behind us.

I know that we may not be able to agree what was the right course for our nation to take in 1966, but we can now agree, I believe, to come together and seek a rebirth of patriotism in which all our citizens can join. We must bind up our wounds. We simply cannot afford to let them fester any longer. The world is too dangerous. We cannot remain distracted from what must be our overriding aim. Our attention must turn to the rebuilding of the military, economic and spiritual foundations of a peaceful world order.

Our people have been shocked and hurt and embarrassed and ashamed over and over again. Things which we used to take for granted are now subject to widespread doubt. Things like trust in our leaders. Confidence in our institutions. Even love and respect for our flag. And support and appreciation for the men and women who served and died for that flag.

But I believe that there is no one in this country, certainly there is no one in this auditorium, who does not want to heal our wounds and restore the precious qualities and the national strengths that we seem to have lost. I hope as President to play a role in that noble enterprise. And I hope that you will help me and my country.

American Legion Convention
Seattle, Washington
August 24, 1976

Coming Home to Iowa

THERE IS no way for me to describe how I feel coming home to Iowa. As Neal Smith was talking about change and opposition to change and agriculture and farmland and historical developments, I thought about two or three weeks ago when I went down to our farm with one of the television network correspondents to the cemetery where our ancestors are buried who were born in 1787. We haven't moved very far since then. And I thought about my own children's great-grandfather who helped to clear that land. He went down into the swamp. He told me when I first came home from the Navy that it was so hot down there that he never wore trousers, just long shirts that came down to about his knees.

He used to plant corn, before it was possible to get a mule and a plow through the new fields, by poking a hole in the ground and dropping in a corn grain and then hoeing around the stalk as it came up. Mr. Captain, as we called him, never did like change either. And I asked Mr. Captain what was the thing that bothered him most, and he said he thought the thing that bothered him most was women's styles. He said when he was a young man women wore their dresses very carefully and that you couldn't even see their instep. Nowadays the dresses don't even cover up their step-ins.

All of us are reluctant to make unnecessary changes, but there are some changes that I have to admit that I like and that happens to be one of them.

This morning I was particularly aware of how many things have changed since the first time that I came to Iowa to campaign. This is where my whole effort started. And I'm grateful to be back with you.

I'll be speaking tomorrow at the State Fair, I'm sure with

several thousand people there, about agriculture, farming. But I remember the first reception we had in Des Moines. We rented a very large hotel ballroom and we had enough food for several hundred people. And four people came. So I stood around embarrassed for a little while—some of the hosts are here with me this afternoon—and then I walked over to the courthouse as Tom Whitney suggested to shake hands.

But my campaign improved from there. We started off with nothing. I come from a little town, 683 people. My wife and I and my children and a few volunteers began to go from one living room to another and from one labor hall to another, and from one shopping center to another, and from one farmers' market and livestock sales barn to another. We made friends, like many of you in this audience, and our campaign grew, and we got known. But it was hard, because in those early days when I would get into a factory shift line, as the workers came by I would shake hands with them and I would say, "I'm Jimmy Carter, I've been Governor of Georgia, I'd like to have your vote. I'm running for President," and by that time they would be almost out of sight. And they'd stop and they'd come back and they'd say, "President of what?"

So by that time I'd lost fifty possible votes. But our campaign grew, and the major contributing factor to my own success was the confidence and the friendship and support that I got in the State of Iowa, and I will never forget it as long as I live.

Democratic Rally, Van Ryswyk Farm
Des Moines, Iowa
August 24, 1976

Peanuts Are a Hard Crop to Grow

SOME OF you are as old as I am. And those of us who have lived on farms for a long time remember how devastating it can be to us if we have a government that doesn't understand us and doesn't care about us. I remember very well growing up during the Hoover depression. Peanuts, as you know, are one of Georgia's most important crops. I remember in 1933 the price for peanuts was one cent a pound.

Now peanuts are a hard crop to grow. But when a farmer with an average allotment of about fifteen acres went out in the field with only his bare hands and a mule and a plow and broke that land, harrowed it at least twice, laid off his rows, went through with the fertilizer distributor and put out the fertilizer, came back later and planted his peanuts, cultivated seven or eight times, pulled every vine of peanuts up out of the ground—they grow like potatoes—shook the dirt off of every vine, put them on a stack pole, let them dry eight or ten weeks until they were dried and cured, and then hauled them to a stationary thrashing machine, separated the peanuts from the vines, put them in his wagon, carried them to market, the total gross income—not net, gross—was seven dollars an acre. You multiply seven dollars an acre by fifteen acres that's a hundred and five dollars a year gross income for farmers during those Hoover depression years. The farm has left a mark on my life. . . .

I want to especially mention, in closing, that I want to improve the life of the rural people of this nation. I live in a little town of Plains, I live on the outskirts of town. We only have 683 people in Plains. Now I don't care if a hundred years from now we still have less than a thousand people who live in Plains. That would suit me fine. But I want to make sure that my children and their children have just as good an education, have just as high a standard of living, have just as much right to control their own lives and their own destiny, as the richest child who lives in the biggest city.

This is the kind of commitment I give to you. That it's time I think in this country for us to form a partnership once again. I hope between me and each one of you individually we can assess the problems of our country and pledge ourselves to correct these problems, and we can listen to the great unanswered questions and provide good answers.

We still have a long way to go. But we can restore in our country the precious things we've lost, the things that still remain strong in rural America. And then all of us can be sure once again that we still live in the greatest nation on earth.

Iowa State Fairgrounds
Des Moines, Iowa
August 25, 1976

"Would You Please Let Me Vote?"

. . . I was elected to the Georgia Senate, my first elected office, in 1962. That was the year the Voter Education Project was organized—1962. One of the first bills on which I had to vote—from a very conservative deep-southwest Georgia county—was to eliminate the notorious "thirty questions" that decided whether or not a Georgian could vote. A white person was given a test on moral character and, of course, very seldom failed. But a black person who came to the same voter registrar was asked thirty questions. And no one in this room could have answered those questions.

And I remember getting up at the Georgia Senate—afraid of the consequences back home—to make a speech for the elimination of that obstacle to the right to vote. And one of my opponents in the debate got up and said, "So many of these people who want to vote are ignorant. How do they know which is the best candidate in the local elections?" And my response was that a black man sitting on the curb outside of the Americus, Georgia, Sumter County Courthouse, who could perhaps have been pushed off by the local sheriff, would be better able to judge who would be a better sheriff than two college professors at Georgia Southwestern College.

We still haven't made enough progress. It is true that in 1962 there were no black legislators in the South. Now there are ninety-five. And even ten years ago, in 1966, there were two hundred black elected officials in the South. Now, there are two thousand. But there has not yet been the realization of our citizens' hopes and dreams nor a demonstration of the correction of years and decades and generations of racial discrimination. We've got a long way to go and it can't be done with a dormant, acquiescent acceptance of a change in the law. It's got to be done with an aggressive, fervent commitment through corrective action, through recruitment, through active registration, through education, through welcoming, to get people who have been excluded from the political process to be part of our nation's life.

Too often decisions are made by those who are powerful and educated and rich and influential and articulate and socially prominent. And even when their hearts are in the right place, and they really want to do a good job of dealing fairly with people, they can't understand the special problems of those who are rural, uneducated, who have some physical or mental defect, who are old, who happen to be black, who can't speak English well, who are timid and inarticulate, and who don't know even what their rights might be.

So we'll never have justice in this country, which we all would like to see, until we have full participation in the political processes for all our people—rich and poor, educated and ignorant, powerful and weak, articulate and timid. That's a challenge for us. Everyone in this room, without exception, can understand what's best for us. If we're wronged, we speak out. We know where to go. We vote regularly. We had no trouble registering to vote. But there are many who look to us for leadership, who don't yet see a realization of the promise that exists in the hearts and minds of our people.

I think the nation's consciousness has been stirred by some of the great leaders that have been chosen in this country in the electoral process. Here in the fifth district, where we are now, with Congressman Andrew Young. In the last election, Harold Ford in Memphis, Tennessee. And Barbara Jordan from Texas, and many others. Mayors, county commissioners, sheriffs. Obviously we've made some progress, and it's given us a new lease on life. We're very proud of it.

But we ought not to be satisfied. I might point out that

this is not just a black, Southern, Democratic type of project. There are many people throughout the country who still feel exclusion that's either deliberate or accepted. We've got four million Spanish-speaking Americans who've never registered to vote. They've seen the high publicity that has accrued to black leaders, civil rights acts, and they feel left out. There are many other white ethnic groups who in the past have not felt they were part of our nation's political process. We ought not to be satisfied just to see the great changes made in the South because of these courageous leaders who preceded most of us and who had courage that we sometimes lacked.

When I came here for the first VEP banquet, I made a brief speech. Nobody paid much attention to it. But for the first time I called for universal voter registration, in May of 1974. In December of 1974 I announced that I was a candidate for President of the United States. And I made a fairly brief speech to the National Press Club in Washington, D. C., and one of the things I called for was universal voter registration. Last month, I made an acceptance speech at the Democratic National Convention in Madison Square Garden and one of the things that was right in the heart of my speech was a call for universal voter registration. If I'm elected President, I want to put John Lewis out of business.

I've talked to a lot of members of Congress who have been adamant in their opposition to postcard registration. And they have told me, "Governor, if we can just pass a law next year that eliminates the red tape, eliminates the cost, eliminates a new bureaucracy, and gets people registered to vote, I'll support it." So one of the commitments I make to you is that whether I'm elected or not I'm going to work hard to see that we have a bill passed in Washington, a very simple bill, that says when somebody is eighteen years old and a citizen of the United States, they're registered to vote.

I believe that this single simple law, which could be written in one paragraph, could almost transform, in a beneficial way, the politics of our country. And the goal for which Martin Luther King, Jr., gave his life, and the goal for which Andy Young and John Lewis were beaten and imprisoned, which is often ignored still many years later, can be realized. I see no reason why a citizen of our country should have to go through a legal process to be given a chance to vote. And I believe this is something we can settle for ourselves. In the meantime let's all join John Lewis and others and give our people a chance to answer a question that they began to ask fifteen or twenty years ago—"Would you please let me vote?"

Voter Education Project
Atlanta, Georgia
August 30, 1976

I Owe the People Everything

Carter delivered his official campaign kickoff speech on Labor Day morning at Franklin Roosevelt's "Little White House" in Warm Springs, Georgia. It was a festive occasion, with thousands of his early supporters packed into the grounds around the Roosevelt home and cheering throughout his remarks. Carter introduced three lines he often used again in his campaign: his "the buck stops here" tribute to Harry Truman, his comparison of his opponent to the captain of a ship that has run aground, and his declaration that "I owe special interests nothing. I owe the people everything."

As I came down the highways that were packed with friends from all over the country, and walked through and shook hands with many of you, I tried to get my thoughts in order for this morning. It's hard to know what to say. It reminds me of the old gentleman who had a reputation for the most vivid vocabulary in the whole community. He had the most choice cuss words that you've ever heard. One day he was moving from one house to another—they just had big rains like last night—and he had to cross a creek in his wagon with all his belongings on it, and some of his neighbors went down to the creek bank, hoping that he would have a mistake, just to enjoy the breadth and scope of his vocabulary.

They all waited with bated breath, and the mules and the wagons got across the creek with no problems, and they were a little disappointed. And as the wagon started up the steep hill, it was kind of rocky, one of the wheels went in a pothole and the old fellow's trunk slipped off the wagon, bounced two or three times over and over, the top came off of it, and it fell in the creek. All his valuables went to the bottom, and all of his clothes drifted slowly down and disappeared in the swamp. And they couldn't wait.

He stood there a long time and he finally shook his head and turned away and said, "There's no way that I can do justice to this situation."

Well, I feel the same way here in Warm Springs this morning.

Warm Springs is a place of history, it's a place of healing, it's a place of leadership. I've got friends in the front row this morning in wheelchairs and using crutches, and they've come here to learn how to make their lives full and useful in public service or in private work. And they demonstrate how courageous achievements are possible in our great country. I love you all.

Today I want to talk about the most famous of all patients who came here looking for a new life. Fifty years ago, in 1926, Franklin Roosevelt purchased Warm Springs, including this historic ground on which we stand. He lived here, he worked here, and he spent his final days right here. Roosevelt first came to Warm Springs because he was physically handicapped. The warm waters gave him strength and hope, and later as President he gave strength and hope to an afflicted nation.

Although he was born into a family with wealth and prominence, Franklin Roosevelt yet understood and served well the millions of American families who were left hopeless and hungry and jobless and despairing by the Great Depression.

His opponent in 1932 was an incumbent President, a decent and well-intentioned man, who felt that the government could not and should not with bold action try to correct the economic ills and the problems of a great nation. He led a Republican Party which lacked the strength to bring us out of those dark days. But Roosevelt knew that our country could do better; and with bold and forceful action he restored confidence to our economic system, he put our nation back to work, and he unified our people. And that changed our lives.

In 1960 another Democratic leader came to Warm Springs. As a candidate, John Kennedy was considered to be an outsider because he was young and because he was relatively inexperienced and because of his religious beliefs. No Catholic had ever been elected President, and some people told Kennedy, "Don't go to Georgia." But he came here, he asked Georgians for our support, and he got more than sixty-two percent of the vote in Georgia, a greater victory than he got even in his own home state of Massachusetts.

This year, as in 1932, our nation is divided, our people are out of work, and our national leaders do not lead.

This year, as in 1960, our nation is drifting without inspiration, without vision, and without purpose. As in those critical years, it is time to restore the faith of American people in their own government and get our country on the move again. This is a year for new ideas and for a new generation of leadership, and that is what we are going to have if you'll help me....

It's obvious what good leadership can do to make a difference. It's also obvious that our government is concerned about special interests now, but when it was concerned about the people the whole nation prospered. The Democratic Party has traditionally provided that kind of leadership. Harry Truman summed up the difference between the two political parties this way, and I quote: "The Republicans believe that the power of government should be used first of all to help the rich and the privileged in the country. With them, property, wealth, comes first. The Democrats believe that the power of government should be used to give the common man more protection and a chance to make a living. With us the people come first."

Harry Truman's words are still true today.

We must also eliminate waste in our government. Scandal and corruption have hit us in recent years like hammer blows. The latest one is the Medicaid program. Designed to give our people better health care, we've now discovered that twenty-five to fifty percent of the billions of dollars in hard-earned tax money is being stolen or wasted. Who's responsible? No one knows. No one knows.

When President Truman was in the White House, there was a sign on his desk. Remember what it said? "The Buck Stops Here." There was never any doubt about who was captain of the ship. Now no one seems to be in charge, no one seems to be responsible. Every time another ship runs aground—the CIA, the FBI, Panama, unemployment, deficits, welfare, inflation, Medicaid—the captain hides in his stateroom and the crew argues about who is to blame. . . .

I want to say just a word about the Soviet Union. We must face the Soviet Union with the hope and the expectation of a constant struggle, but without the use of arms. A continuing peaceful competition. I'm not afraid of that kind of competition, in fact I look forward to it, but we've got to have our own system working here at home. We've got to have trust of people in government. We've got to have our people working together. We've got to have a clear vision of what we want to do. We've got to have good leadership. We need not be afraid. Our economic strength, our system of government, the character and freedom of our people, are tremendous resources that are waiting to be tapped. But now our country is stagnant. It's drifting. It's divided. It's time for a change. We must be united and strong, we must get our nation on the move again.

I want to close by saying this. I'll try to be a good candidate, and if I'm elected I'll try to be a worthy leader of our great country. During my entire lifetime, from farm boy to nominee of the Democratic Party for President of the United

States, I've always been close to the working families of this nation.

As a political candidate I owe special interests nothing. I owe the people everything.

We now stand just a few miles from my home. My friends in this audience and my family and I have campaigned throughout the United States. We've covered almost every part of our country. We've been in private homes and we've heard the voices and the encouragement and the advice and criticism of people like you everywhere. That's where our political strength has been derived. We've never let powerful intermediaries stand between me and the people. To whatever degree I can stay close to you and depend on you, derive my strength from you, my advice and counsel and criticism from you, to that extent my campaign for President will be successful and to that extent I will be a good President of this country.

We've come a long way. We still have a long way to go. As in 1932 and in 1960, the choice before our people is clear. Are we Americans satisfied with a divided nation, one of timidity, confusion, and mediocrity? Most of us believe that we can do better. We'll be proud to work hard together and to sacrifice, if necessary, to achieve once again a united country, a nation of faith, a nation of vision, a nation of courage, and a nation of greatness.

The Little White House
Warm Springs, Georgia
September 6, 1976

Human Rights

I AM proud to meet with a group of men and women with whom I share a total commitment to the preservation of human rights, individual liberty, and freedom of conscience.

I would like to talk to you about my view of how our nation should encourage and support those priceless qualities throughout the world. This is, as you know, a difficult question. It requires a great deal of balancing between idealism and realism, of our understanding of the world as it is and our understanding of the world as it ought to be.

The question, I think, is whether in recent years our highest officials have not been too pragmatic, even cynical, and as a consequence have ignored those moral values that have often distinguished our own country from other nations around the world.

Our greatest source of strength has always come from basic priceless values, our belief in the freedom of religion, our belief in the freedom of speech and expression, our belief in human dignity, our belief in the principle of simple justice. These principles have made us great, and unless our foreign policy reflects these principles we make a mockery of the celebration of our two hundredth birthday as we look back to the ideals and hopes of those who founded our great country.

We have not always lived up to our ideals, but I know of no great nation on earth that has more often conducted itself in a moral, unselfish manner abroad, and which has provided more freedom and opportunity to its own citizens at home.

Still, in recent years there has been a gap between values that we have proclaimed and the policies that we have pursued.

We have often become militarily entangled in the internal

166

affairs of distant countries. Our government has pursued dubious tactics, and the phrase "national security" has sometimes been a cover-up for unnecessary scandals and for unnecessary secrecy.

We stumbled into the quagmires of Vietnam and Cambodia, and we carried out heavy-handed efforts to destroy an elected government in Chile. In Cyprus we let expediency triumph over fairness, and we lost both ways. We responded inadequately to human suffering in places like Bangladesh, Burundi, the Sahel, and other undeveloped areas of the world.

We lessened the prestige of our foreign ambassadors by sending abroad men and women who were distinguished only by the size of their political contributions to a successful President.

We have allowed the almost completely unrestricted sale of military weapons around the world, a policy that is as cynical as it is dangerous.

I find it unacceptable that we have, in effect, condoned the effort of some Arab countries to tell American businesses that in order to trade with one country or one company, that they must observe restrictions based on race or religion. These so-called Arab boycotts violate our basic standards of freedom and morality and they must be stopped—period.

We also regret our own government's continuing failure to oppose the denial of freedom in Eastern Europe and in the Soviet Union. The Republican administration has shown a lack of sensitivity to the craving of Eastern European people for greater independence. That also is unacceptable.

Only thirteen months ago, President Ford and Henry Kissinger traveled to Helsinki to sign a treaty of comprehensive security and cooperation. It was supposed to lead to greater personal freedom, according to the agreement written, for the people of Eastern Europe and for the Soviet Union, including greater freedom to travel, to marry, and

to emigrate; but since that elaborate signing ceremony in
Finland, the Russians have ignored their pledge, and the
Ford administration has looked away. Similarly, the Ameri-
can government has failed to make serious efforts to get the
Russians to permit greater numbers of people to emigrate
freely to the countries of their choice. We cannot pass over
in silence the deprivation of human rights in the Soviet
Union. The list of Soviet prisoners is long, both Jewish and
Christian. I will speak only of two as examples. Vladimir
Bukovsky, and Vladimir Slepak.

Bukovsky is a young scientist who has been in prison most
of the last thirteen years for criticisms of the Soviet regime.
Slepak, a radio engineer in Moscow, applied for an exit visa
in 1970 to go to the nation of Israel. The visa was denied,
and since 1972 he has been denied the right to hold a job.

I ask, Why have such people been deprived of their basic
rights, a full year after Helsinki? If I become President, the
fate of men like Bukovsky and Slepak will be very much on
my mind as I negotiate with the Soviet Union, and you can
also depend on that.

Of course, we all know that liberty is sometimes denied in
some non-communist countries too. Many cases of political
persecution in Chile and reports of brutal torture are too well
documented to be disbelieved. There are those governments,
such as in South Korea, which openly violate human rights,
although they themselves are under threats from communist
regimes which represent an even greater level of repression.
Even in such cases, however, we should not condone repression or the denial of freedom. On the contrary, we should
use our tremendous influence to increase freedom, particularly in those countries that depend upon us for their very
survival.

Denials of human rights, as you know perhaps better than
any other people, occur in many places and in many ways. In
Ireland, for instance, violence has bred more violence, and

caused untold human suffering, which brings sorrow to the entire civilized world.

I do not say to you that these are simple issues. I do not say to you that we can remake the world in our own image. I recognize the limits on our power, but the present administration—our government—has been so obsessed with balance-of-power politics that it has often ignored basic American values and a common and proper concern for human rights. The leaders of this administration have often rationalized that there is little room for morality in foreign affairs and that we must put self-interest above principle. I disagree strongly, and I know you join me in that disagreement.

Ours is a great and a powerful nation, committed to certain enduring ideals, and those ideals must be reflected not only in our domestic policy but also in our foreign policy. There are practical, effective ways in which our power can be used to alleviate human suffering around the world. We should begin by having it understood that if any nation, whatever its political system, deprives its own people of basic human rights, that fact will help shape our own people's attitude toward that nation's repressive government. If other nations want our friendship and support, they must understand that we want to see basic human rights respected by all governments.

Now I know that our power is not unlimited, but it is not insignificant either; and I believe that if we are sensitive, and if we are openly and constantly concerned, there can be many instances when our power can make a crucial difference in the lives of thousands of men and women who have been the victims of oppression around the world. Now we must be realistic. Although we believe deeply in our own system of government, and in our own ideals, we do not and should not insist on identical standards or an identical system of government in all nations. We can live with diversity in governmental systems, but we cannot look away when a government tortures people or jails them for their beliefs or denies minorities fair treatment or the right to emigrate.

Let me suggest some additional actions that our government should take in the area of human rights. First, we can support the principle of self-determination by refraining from military intervention in the domestic politics of other countries.

We should not behave abroad in ways that violate our own laws and our own moral standards. You and I would not plot murder or assassination, but in recent years officials of my government and your government have plotted murder and assassinations that are obviously wrong and unacceptable.

In giving trade assistance or economic assistance to other governments, we should make sure that the aid is used to benefit the people of that country. There will be times when we will want to help those who must live under a repressive government. We may refrain from giving general economic aid or military assistance to a government, and yet wish to provide food, health care, or other humanitarian assistance directly to the people themselves.

The United States should give more vigorous support to the United Nations and to other international bodies in order to attract world attention to the denial of freedom. These bodies are limited in power, and I believe that's best; but they can serve as a conscience of the world community, and they deserve far more support than our government has given them in recent years.

These questions are important to you. These questions are important to me. These questions are important to the people I have visited in the last twenty-four hours in Connecticut and New York, in Philadelphia and Scranton and Pittsburgh, in my own State of Georgia, and they are important to the people around the world who look to the United States of America for guidance and for a standard of morality and commitment to human freedom.

When we are quiet or timid or without leadership, this circumstance saps away the commitment of other free people to those basic principles.

I have outlined to you today a few of the things that our nation can do for a change to promote rights in our imperfect world. The basic question is one of leadership. In foreign affairs, and also in domestic affairs, we need leaders who are not only concerned with the powerless, with the weak, with the disfranchised, with the persecuted, and with the victims of oppression throughout this globe. We have not had that kind of leadership in the White House in recent years. If I am elected President, I intend to provide that leadership.

B'nai B'rith Convention
Washington, D.C.
September 8, 1976

Once the People Rule Again

... I UNDERSTAND that my opponent made his kickoff speech today in Michigan, and some people say that tonight marks the official start of the campaign of 1976.

I'm glad to see his final and reluctant emergence from the Rose Garden, but I think in a larger sense this presidential campaign began a long time ago. My opponent and I and the two parties we represent do not exist in isolation. We are part of the currents of history.

In that sense this campaign was under way in 1932, when his party nominated Herbert Hoover and ours nominated Franklin Roosevelt.

As you may know, I started my campaign last week in Warm Springs. Warm Springs was purchased by Roosevelt in 1926, fifty years ago. His life had almost been destroyed by polio, and he went down there to restore his soul and body, to pray and to think and to plan for the future. And he ran for President in 1932 against Herbert Hoover, a decent man, a well-intentioned man perhaps, but who didn't see that his responsibility was to try to ease the handicap of people who were without jobs and were without hope and were discouraged.

But Roosevelt moved forward in the tradition of the Democratic Party. He had confidence in us and he helped us. He proposed a twenty-five-cent-an-hour minimum wage. Twenty-five cents. The Democratic Congress finally passed it, but ninety-five percent of the Republicans in Congress voted against it.

He gave Rural Electrification to farm homes like mine. He thought people ought to have security in their old age and he put forward Social Security. There were ninety-five Republican House members, and ninety-four voted against Social Security. That draws a distinct difference between this good man, Franklin Roosevelt, in the tradition of the Democratic Party, and Herbert Hoover, in the tradition of the Republican Party.

That's when this campaign began, and this campaign continued in 1948, when his party, Ford's, nominated Thomas Dewey, and ours nominated Harry Truman.

Harry Truman was a common man like many of you, and like myself, but he was an uncommon President. He understood us and he was courageous. He made tough decisions, he never backed off, he never separated from us. I never thought he told us a lie.

He didn't hesitate when he came to Point Four, NATO, the Marshall Plan, aid to Turkey and Greece, recognizing Israel, setting up the United Nations, dealing with businessmen, workers, when lives were at stake. He had a sign on his desk in the Oval Office. Does anybody remember what it said?

"The buck stops here."

We knew that he was President. Nowadays the buck can run all over Washington looking for a place to stop. Nobody is in charge, nobody is responsible—for Watergate, CIA, unemployment, inflation, the Medicaid scandal—nobody's in charge. That's in the tradition of the Republican Party.

Our campaign continued in 1952, when his party nominated Dwight Eisenhower and ours nominated Adlai Stevenson.

This campaign continued in 1960, when his party nominated Richard Nixon and ours nominated John Fitzgerald Kennedy.

John Kennedy also came to Warm Springs, Georgia; it was his only stop in our region. His staff said, "Don't go there, because Georgia is a conservative state, lot of Protestants, they don't know you, you're a liberal, you're from Boston," but John Kennedy came down to Warm Springs and made one speech. He asked the Georgia people to give him our support, and when the returns came in in November of 1960, John Fitzgerald Kennedy got his biggest margin of victory not in Massachusetts but in the State of Georgia, and I'm proud of that.

Our campaign continued in 1964, when President Ford's party nominated Barry Goldwater and ours nominated Lyndon Johnson.

This campaign continued in 1968, when his party nominated Richard Nixon a second time and ours nominated Hubert Humphrey.

The campaign continued in 1972, when his party turned again for a third time to Richard Nixon and ours nominated George McGovern.

We haven't won all those elections, but the point is if you look at the difference between the parties and what they stand for, judge by the nominees, there's a continuum there, a constant reminder to the working people of this country about which party, which candidates are best for you.

This campaign has been joined a hundred times over, whenever our party has fought for legislation that would benefit the average American—for Social Security, for minimum wage laws, for Rural Electrification, for voting rights, for civil rights, for Medicare—and our opponent's party has fought against all that progress.

This year the lines are drawn with special clarity. For my opponent, in his long career in Congress, has distinguished himself not by any legislation that I can recall that bears his name, a Congressional record that equals his record at the White House, but his tireless opposition to all the great legislation that bears the name of Democrats that cared for people, and who were not controlled by special interests.

There has never been an American election quite like this one. We've had economic problems before, we've had poor leadership before, but we've never had such widespread lack of trust among the American people in their own government.

Because of a war our people did not want, because of scandal our people did not want, because of economic mismanagement that our people did not want, millions of Americans have lost faith in government.

We feel that we've lost control of our own government, that it has become our master instead of our servant, that we are being ruled by special interests and by politicians who just don't care about us. To a tragic degree that's exactly what has happened.

That's what this campaign is all about. We as Democrats must give our people faith in our own government again by giving our people control over our government once again.

Government by the people—that's the issue this year.

Once the people rule again, we can solve our economic problems, put our people back to work, cut inflation, and with growth have balanced budgets and good services for all.

Once the people rule again, we can have a fair tax system for a change.

Once the people rule again, we can reorganize our government and make it work with competence and with compassion, with a good welfare program and comprehensive health care.

Once the people rule again, we can have a foreign policy to make us proud.

It all depends on the people.

That is why we're going to win in November. Because we've always gone to the people, because we've always listened to the people, because we've always learned from the people, because we take our strength and our hope and our courage from the people.

I owe special interests nothing. I owe the people everything. And I'm going to keep it that way.

So let's go forth on this campaign gladly and proudly and

bravely. Let us go forth in the spirit of Franklin Roosevelt and John Kennedy and Harry Truman and Lyndon Johnson and all the others that have made us proud to be Democrats.

And let us always put our faith in the American people, for as long as we do, no power on earth can ever prevail against us in the greatest nation on earth.

AFL-CIO Convention
Dearborn, Michigan
September 15, 1976

But I Don't Think the People Will Be Fooled

... I'D JUST like to say one word about agriculture. One of the reasons that I get up early every morning—five or six days a week—and put in sixteen hours campaigning is so that January twentieth, 1977, I can send Earl Butz back where he came from.

The day before yesterday I spoke to about seventy thousand people at the Farmfest in Minnesota. Earl Butz was there the day before I was. And he predicted to the crowd —there were only a couple of hundred folks, I understand, and he couldn't draw that big a crowd in Georgia—but he predicted to the crowd that when I arrived that I was going to announce that when I was elected President he would be fired. That's the first accurate prediction that Earl Butz has made in a long time.

I made a speech last spring to the Gridiron Club in Washington, and my good friend Earl Butz was there and he walked up to me and he said, "Governor, I understand that everywhere you go you promise that you are going to fire me if you are elected."

I said, "Yes sir, that's right."

"But why do you have to say it more than once?" he asked.

I said, "Well, first of all, that's my best applause line. Also, in a lot of places in the country, the farmers are very discouraged, and it gives them something to look forward to next year."

The other night, my opponent reluctantly emerged from the Rose Garden and finally made his first speech of the campaign. He spoke of his vision of America. And it was a fine vision, a noble vision. The only trouble was that my opponent has spent his entire life in politics opposing the programs that could make the vision come true.

He seems to have experienced in the last few weeks a remarkable conversion at this late date in his political life.

But I don't think the people will be fooled. Mr. Ford cannot rhapsodize about the future as if he and his party had no past. The Republican Party, from Hoover and McKinley and Coolidge to Nixon, has been the party of negativism and opposition, the party that at every turn had to be dragged kicking and screaming from the past into the present. The Democratic Party, the party of Roosevelt and Truman and John Kennedy and Lyndon Johnson, is a party that has a genuine vision for America and has always fought to make that vision a reality.

Rally
Hot Springs, Arkansas
September 17, 1976

From the Playboy Interview

The *Playboy* interview was conducted in bits and pieces over a three-month period in the spring and summer of 1976. The interviewer, Robert Scheer, pressed Carter hard on his alleged piety and moralism, until finally, at the conclusion of their last interview, Carter declared that he didn't consider himself any better than another man just because the other man might "screw" or "shack up" with women outside of marriage. The interview was made public on September 20, and Carter's choice of language caused a great furor. For a week or two Carter's words seemed to be the major issue in the presidential campaign. The controversy over Carter's closing remarks obscured the many revealing remarks Carter made to Scheer in the body of the interview. The following are some highlights of their exchange.

PLAYBOY: . . . Isn't it true that you turned out to be more liberal as governor of Georgia than people who voted for you had any reason to suspect?

CARTER: I don't really think so. No, *The Atlanta Constitution*, which was the source of all information about me, categorized me during the gubernatorial campaign as an ignorant, racist, backward, ultraconservative, rednecked South Georgia peanut farmer. Its candidate, Carl Sanders, the former governor, was characterized as an enlightened, progressive, well-educated, urbane, forceful, competent public official. I never agreed with the categorization that was made of me during the campaign. I was the same person before and after I became governor. I remember keeping a check list and every time I made a promise during the campaign, I wrote it down in a notebook. I believe I carried out every promise I made. I told several people during the campaign that one of the phrases I was going to use in my inaugural speech was that the time for racial discrimination was over. I wrote and made that speech. . . .

PLAYBOY: Considering what you've just said about *The Atlanta Constitution,* how do you feel about the media in general and about the job they do in covering the election issues?

CARTER: . . . Issues? The local media are interested, all right, but the national news media have absolutely no interest in issues *at all.* Sometimes we freeze out the national media so we can open up press conferences to local people. At least we get questions from them—on timber management, on health care, on education. But the traveling press have zero interest in any issue unless it's a matter of making a mistake. What they're looking for is a 47-second argument between me and another candidate or something like that. There's nobody in the back of this plane who would ask an issue question unless he thought he could trick me into some crazy statement.

PLAYBOY: While we're on the subject of the press, how do you feel about an issue that concerns the press itself—the right of journalists to keep their sources secret?

CARTER: I would do everything I could to protect the secrecy of sources for the news media.

PLAYBOY: Both the press *and* the public seem to have made an issue out of your Baptist beliefs. Why do you think this has happened?

CARTER: I'm not unique. There are a lot of people in this country who have the same religious faith. It's not a mysterious or mystical or magical thing. But for those who don't know the feeling of someone who believes in Christ, who is aware of the presence of God, there is, I presume, a quizzical attitude toward it. But it's always been something I've discussed very frankly throughout my adult life.

PLAYBOY: We've heard that you pray 25 times a day. Is that true?

CARTER: I've never counted. I've forgotten who asked me that, but I'd say that on an eventful day, you know, it's something like that.

PLAYBOY: When you say an eventful day, do you mean you pray as a kind of pause, to control your blood pressure and relax?

CARTER: Well, yes. If something happens to me that is a little disconcerting, if I feel trepidation, if a thought comes into my head of animosity or hatred toward someone, then I just kind of say a brief silent prayer. I don't ask for myself but just to let me understand what another's feelings might be. Going through a crowd, quite often people bring me a problem, and I pray that their needs might be met. A lot of times, I'll be in the back seat of a car and not know what kind of audience I'm going to face. I don't mean I'm terror-stricken, just that I don't know what to expect next. I'll pray then, but it's not something that's conscious or formal. It's just a part of my life.

PLAYBOY: . . . we still wonder how *your* religious beliefs would translate into political action. For instance, would you appoint judges who would be harsh or lenient toward victimless crimes—offenses such as drug use, adultery, sodomy and homosexuality?

CARTER: Committing adultery, according to the Bible—which I believe in—is a sin. For us to hate one another, for us to have sexual intercourse outside marriage, for us to engage in homosexual activities, for us to steal, for us to lie—all these are sins. But Jesus teaches us not to judge other people. We don't assume the role of judge and say to another human being, "You're condemned because you commit sins." All Christians, all of us, acknowledge that we are sinful and the judgment comes from God, not from another human being. As governor of Georgia, I tried to shift the emphasis of law enforcement away from victimless crimes. We lessened the penalties on the use of marijuana. We removed alcoholism as a crime, and so forth. Victimless crimes, in my opinion, should have a very low priority in terms of enforcing the laws on the books. But as to appointing judges, that would not be the basis on which I'd appoint them. I would choose people who were competent, whose judgment and integrity were sound. I think it would be inappropriate to ask them how they were going to rule on a particular question before I appointed them.

PLAYBOY: Do you think liberalization of the laws over the past decade by factors as diverse as the pill and PLAYBOY— an effect some people would term permissiveness—has been a harmful development?

CARTER: Liberalization of some of the laws has been good. You can't legislate morality. We tried to outlaw consumption of alcoholic beverages. We found that violation of the law led to bigger crimes and bred disrespect for the law.

PLAYBOY: What we're getting at is how much you'd tolerate behavior that your religion considers wrong. For instance, in San Francisco, you said you considered homosexuality a sin. What does that mean in political terms?

CARTER: The issue of homosexuality always makes me nervous. It's obviously one of the major issues in San Francisco. I don't have any, you know, personal knowledge about homosexuality and I guess being a Baptist, that would contribute to a sense of being uneasy.

PLAYBOY: We'd like to ask you a blunt question: Isn't it just these views about what's "sinful" and what's "immoral" that contribute to the feeling that you might get a call from God, or get inspired and push the wrong button? More realistically, wouldn't we expect a puritanical tone to be set in the White House if you were elected?

CARTER: Harry Truman was a Baptist. Some people get very abusive about the Baptist faith. If people want to know about it, they can read the New Testament. The main thing is that we don't think we're better than anyone else. We are taught not to judge other people. But as to some of the behavior you've mentioned, I can't change the teachings of Christ. I can't change the teachings of Christ! I believe in them, and a lot of people in this country do as well. Jews believe in the Bible. They have the same commandments.

PLAYBOY: Then you as President, in appointing Supreme Court Justices—

CARTER: I think we've pursued this conversation long enough —if you have another question. . . . Look, I'll try to express my views. It's not a matter of condemnation, it's not a matter of persecution. I've been a governor for four years. Anybody can come and look at my record. I didn't run around breaking down people's doors to see if they were fornicating. This is something that's ridiculous.

PLAYBOY: We know you didn't, but we're being so persistent because of this matter of self-righteousness, because of the moral certainty of so many of your statements. People wonder if Jimmy Carter ever is unsure. Has he ever been wrong, has he ever had a failure of moral nerve?

CARTER: Well, there are a lot of things I could have done differently had I known during my early life what I now know. I would certainly have spoken out more clearly and loudly on the civil rights issue. I would have demanded that our nation never get involved initially in the Vietnam war. I would have told the country in 1972 that Watergate was a much more horrible crime than we thought at the time. It's easy to say in hindsight what you would have done if you had had information you now have. . . .

PLAYBOY: What about Chile? Would you agree that that was a case of the United States', through the CIA, intervening improperly?

CARTER: Yes. There's no doubt about it. Sure.

PLAYBOY: And you would stop that sort of thing?

CARTER: Absolutely. Yes, sir.

PLAYBOY: To what do you attribute all those deceptions and secret maneuverings through the years? Why were they allowed to happen?

CARTER: It was a matter of people's just saying, Well, that's politics; we don't have a right to know what our Government is doing; secrecy is OK; accepting gifts is OK; excluding the American people is OK. These are the kinds of things I want to change.

PLAYBOY: It sounds as if you're saying Americans accepted indecency and lies in their Government all too easily. Doesn't that make your constant campaign theme, invoking the decency and honesty of the American people, somewhat naïve and ingenuous?

CARTER: I say that the American people are basically decent and honest and want a truthful Government. Obviously, I know there are people in this country, out of 214,000,000, who are murderers. There are people, maybe, who don't want a decent Government. Maybe there are people who prefer lies to truth. But I don't think it's simplistic to say that our Government hasn't measured up to the ethical and moral standards of the people of this country. We've had better governments in the past and I think our people, as I've said many times, are just as strong, courageous and intelligent as they were 200 years ago. I think we still have the same inner strength they had then.

PLAYBOY: Even though a lot of people support that feeling, many others think it makes you sound like an evangelist. And that makes it all the more confusing when they read about your hanging out with people so different from you in lifestyle and beliefs. Your publicized friendship with journalist Hunter Thompson, who makes no secret of his affinity for drugs and other craziness, is a good example.

CARTER: Well, in the first place, I'm a human being. I'm not a packaged article that you can put in a little box and say,

"Here's a Southern Baptist, an ignorant Georgia peanut farmer who doesn't have the right to enjoy music, who has no flexibility in his mind, who can't understand the sensitivities of an interpersonal relationship. He's gotta be predictable. He's gotta be for Calley and for the war. He's gotta be a liar. He's gotta be a racist."

You know, that's the sort of stereotype people tend to assume, and I hope it doesn't apply to me. And I don't see any mystery about having a friendship with Hunter Thompson. I guess it's something that's part of my character and it becomes a curiosity for those who see some mystery about someone of my background being elected President. I'm just a human being like everybody else. I have different interests, different understandings of the world around me, different relationships with different kinds of people. I have a broad range of friends: sometimes very serious, sometimes very formal, sometimes lighthearted, sometimes intense, sometimes casual.

PLAYBOY: So when you find yourself at a rock concert or in some other situation that seems at odds with your rural, religious background, you never feel a sense of estrangement?

CARTER: None. No. I feel at home with 'em.

PLAYBOY: How did you get to feel this way without going through culture shock?

CARTER: I have three sons, who now range from 23 to 29, and the oldest of them were very influenced by Bob Dylan in their attitudes toward civil rights, criminal justice and the Vietnam war. This was about the period of time I was entering politics. I've been fairly close to my sons and their taste in music influenced my taste, and I was able to see the impact of Bob Dylan's attitudes on young people. And I was both gratified by and involved emotionally in those changes of attitudes.

PLAYBOY: Let us ask you about one last stand: abortion.

CARTER: I think abortion is wrong and I will do everything I can as President to minimize the need for abortions—within the framework of the decision of the Supreme Court, which I can't change. Georgia had a more conservative approach to abortion, which I personally favored, but the Supreme Court ruling suits me all right. I signed a Georgia law as governor that was compatible with the Supreme Court decision.

PLAYBOY: You think it's wrong, but the ruling suits you? What would we tell a woman who said her vote would depend on how you stood on abortion?

CARTER: If a woman's major purpose in life is to have unrestricted abortions, then she ought not to vote for me. But she wouldn't have anyone to vote for. . . .

PLAYBOY: You mention very frequently how much you count on your wife's advice. Isn't there a strain during the campaign, with the two of you separated so much of the time?

CARTER: Well, when I was in the Navy, I was at sea most of the time and I'd see her maybe one or two nights a week. Now, when I'm home in Plains, I see her almost every night. And if I'm elected President, I'll see her *every* night. So there is obviously a time to be together and a time to be separated. If you're apart three or four days and then meet again, it's almost—for me, it's a very exciting reunion. I'll have been away from Rosalynn for a few days and if I see her across an airport lobby, or across a street, I get just as excited as I did when I was, you know, 30 years younger.

We have a very close, very intimate sharing of our lives and we've had a tremendous magnification of our life's purposes in politics. Before 1966, she and I were both very shy. It was almost a painful thing to approach a stranger or make a speech. It's been a mutual change we've gone through, because we both felt it was worth while; so no matter what the outcome of the election, the relationship between Rosalynn and me will be very precious. . . .

PLAYBOY: This is a tough question to ask, but because it's been such a factor in American political life, we wonder if you've ever discussed with Rosalynn the possibility of being assassinated. And, assuming you have, how do you deal with it in your own mind?

CARTER: Well, in the first place, I'm not afraid of death. In the second place, it's the same commitment I made when I volunteered to go into the submarine force. I accepted a certain degree of danger when I made the original decision, then I didn't worry about it anymore. It wasn't something that preyed on my mind; it wasn't something I had to reassess every five minutes. There is a certain element of danger in running for President, borne out by statistics on the number of Presidents who have been attacked, but I have to say frankly that it's something I never worry about.

PLAYBOY: Your first answer was that you don't fear death. Why not?

CARTER: It's part of my religious belief. I just look at death as not a threat. It's inevitable, and I have an assurance of eternal life. There is no feeling on my part that I *have* to be President, or that I *have* to live, or that I'm immune to danger. It's just that the termination of my physical life is relatively insignificant in my concept of over-all existence. I don't say that in a mysterious way; I recognize the possibility of assassination. But I guess everybody recognizes the possibility of other forms of death—automobile accidents, airplane accidents, cancer. I just don't worry. . . .

PLAYBOY: Thanks for all the time you've given us. Incidentally, do you have any problems with appearing in PLAYBOY? Do you think you'll be criticized?

CARTER: I don't object to that at all. I don't believe I'll be criticized.

Playboy
November 1976

Closing Statement, First Carter–Ford Debate

TONIGHT WE have had a chance to talk a lot about the past, but I think it is time to talk about the future.

Our nation in the last eight years has been divided as never before. It is a time for unity. It is a time to draw ourselves together, to have a President and a Congress that can work together, with mutual respect for a change, cooperating for a change, and in the open for a change, so that the people can understand their own government. It is time for government, industry, labor, manufacturing, agriculture, education, other entities of our society, to cooperate. It is a time for government to understand and to cooperate with our people.

For a long time our American citizens have been excluded —sometimes misled, sometimes lied to. This is not compatible with the purpose of our nation. I believe in our country. It needs to be competent. The government needs to be well managed, efficient, economical. We need to have a government that is sensitive to our people's needs—to those who are poor, who don't have adequate health care, who have been cheated too long with our tax programs, who have been out of jobs, whose families have been torn apart. We need to restore the faith and the trust of the American people in their own government.

In addition to that, we have suffered because we haven't had leadership in this Administration. We have a government of stalemate. We have lost the vision of what our country can and ought to be. This is not the America that we have known in the past. It is not the America that we have to have in the future.

I don't claim to know all the answers. But I have got confidence in my country. Our economic strength is still there.

Our system of government—in spite of Vietnam, Cambodia, CIA, Watergate—is still the best system of government on earth. And the greatest resource of all is the 215 million Americans who still have within us the strength, the character, the intelligence, the experience, patriotism, the idealism, the compassion, the sense of brotherhood, on which we can rely in the future to restore the greatness to our country.

We ought not to be excluded from our government anymore. We need a President to go in who derives his strength from the people. I owe the special interests nothing. I owe everything to you, the people of this country.

I believe we can bind our wounds. I believe that we can work together. And I believe that we can tap the tremendous untapped reservoir of innate strength in this country. And we can once again have a government as good as our people, and let the world know what we still know and hope for— that we still live in the greatest and the strongest and the best country on earth.

Philadelphia, Pennsylvania
September 23, 1976

I Can't Win Without You

TODAY I want to talk about two things: leadership and people.

Think about a father proud like you are, competent like you are, self-reliant like you are. The head of a household like many of you, or a mother eager to work but can't find a job.

They come home at night, face the children with the authority and the responsibility and the respect that should go to the breadwinner stripped away. Put yourself in that position. Think of going down and drawing your first welfare check when you've worked all your life. It tears a family apart. It destroys their self-respect. It eliminates basic human dignity. And in the last two years, two and a half million more Americans have had to accept that circumstance.

Let's look at inflation. When it was announced that the inflation rate was only six percent, President Ford and his press secretary said, "That's great, just six percent." And when Johnson and Kennedy were in office before the Vietnam war, the inflation rate was three percent. When Harry Truman went out of office, it was less than one percent. A six percent inflation rate comes in and steals the ability of a family to be held together. Older people with fixed incomes fear the day that their lives are squeezed. An elderly person on a fixed retirement check buys inferior food, maybe has to leave one's own home, can't buy a new dress every year. And when Christmas time comes, if they can give their grandchildren a present it's a cheap present. That's a debilitating circumstance.

Families that have been wise and prudent and worked hard and saved their money and put it in a savings account—five percent interest—find that every year they've lost one percent on their life's savings. This is not the kind of nation that we want. It is not the kind of nation that we must have.

Crime is something that's increased so greatly in the last few years it's almost inconceivable.

The CIA has spied on our own people. The FBI has committed burglaries. I remember the time up until recently that when you said the three letters FBI your heart kind of lifted up with pride. There is an institution of professionals who protect my life and who protect my property. And we thought they would never do anything that was shameful. But lately it's changed. And it hurts us all; that attitude comes down throughout our society.

The unemployment rate contributes to crime. The overloaded judicial system contributes to crime. The thing that hurts too is the realization that if you don't have influence, if you're poor, an average member of a working American family, and you commit a crime, you've got a good chance of going to prison. But if you're rich, you'll never see the inside of a prison in this country.

And that's not right. I'm not trying to send rich people to prison, but the point I make is that there ought not to be a double standard.

The American people are fair. Our system of justice is not fair.

The American people are honest. Our government hasn't been honest.

The American people believe in work. We've developed in recent years a welfare government.

The American people believe in tough, competent management. We've seen evolve a bloated, confused, bureaucratic mess.

The American people believe that we ought to control our government. On the other hand we've seen government more and more controlling us.

These things are not part of the consciousness of Texans or Americans.

This is a time for change in our country. I don't want the people to change. I want the government to change. I can't win without you. It's going to be a tough, hard-fought political contest. I look forward to it. Texas, Dallas, are difficult for a Democrat to carry, as you know, but particularly to defeat, as an outsider, an incumbent President with a unified party. I can't do it without you.

Democratic Reception
Dallas, Texas
September 24, 1976

From an Interview with Norman Mailer for
The New York Times Magazine

MAILER: Just testing it, just testing it.

CARTER: I see you came well prepared this morning.

MAILER: Yesterday, when I left, I was ashamed that I hadn't really done the homework.

CARTER: You know, I felt that perhaps the church service was disconcerting to you to some degree.

MAILER: Well, I went away afterward and I thought, Mr. Carter's at least as much of an engineer as he is a mystic.

CARTER: That's not much of a mystic!

MAILER: ... You must be a good athlete then.

CARTER: No, no, I'm not a very good athlete.

MAILER: But you're certainly not a bad one?

CARTER: I'm fairly well-coordinated. In the Naval Academy, I went out for cross-country, and played on the 140-pound football team, and I can play softball and basketball and baseball and I'm a fairly good quail hunter and I know how to fish and I can handle a canoe in rough water.

MAILER: Can you handle a rifle?

CARTER: Pretty good. Good pistol shot.

MAILER: I've got time I guess for two more questions. One of them is just to verify something you said yesterday. You mentioned that your sons had had about as much acquaintance with drugs as any other American boy. Would this be a fair way to put it?

CARTER: Well, I wouldn't say "as much as any other American boy," but they've all experimented with marijuana, and they've been associated with friends who are much more deeply involved in this drug culture. Yes, they are thoroughly familiar with it. That's right. The point I was making was they got over it because they had a kind of a stable family and they got married earlier and their wives gave them a little more stability in life and they got away from it. But when we put into effect the hard-drug treatment program in Georgia, my sons could work with drug addicts with a feeling of understanding and compatibility.

MAILER: I have a daughter who started taking it in college for a while. I say to all my kids, look, I'm not going to pretend you're not going to enjoy it. But don't start smoking until after you've had your education. What marijuana tends to do is make your mind run downhill. You run together all the things you've learned, and that's a lot of fun. But don't take it while you're getting your education, for you'll have nothing afterward to put together.

CARTER: Did they take your advice?

MAILER: Uh, not particularly, no.

CARTER: Mine didn't either.

MAILER: I was married to a young lady from Georgia once, and I happened to be talking to her before I left, and she said, you be sure to ask Governor Carter if he knows my family, the Kendricks; they're in peanuts, too.

CARTER: Sure, I know the Kendricks. As a matter of fact, my Uncle Alton's wife is a Kendrick.

MAILER: Your uncle, I better write that down.

CARTER: You ought to go by and talk to him. You know where the antique store is downtown? Well, it's right there. My uncle Alton Carter, he's my father's only brother and his wife, Betty, whom he married after his first wife died, she's from the Kendrick family. She could tell you about the family background. Where does your ex-wife live now?

MAILER: She lives in Provincetown.

CARTER: Well, that's a beautiful place.

MAILER: Provincetown?

CARTER: Yes.

MAILER: You've been there?

CARTER: Rosalynn and I spent a delightful period up there when I was putting the U.S.S. K-1 in commission, the first ship they built after the war.

MAILER: You and Rosalynn lived in Provincetown?

CARTER: Just briefly during the sea trials. I remember one night we got an enormous lobster, seems to me now it must have been about 12 pounds. Even everyone who lived there was remarking about how large it was. We all cooked that lobster and ate it. We had a delightful time. The artists were there, you know, and there was a bar down there on the end, I can remember they used to serve beer in enormous buckets and we would go in and sing and we had a black guy on our submarine and he was the best softball pitcher I've ever seen in my life. His name was Russell and he had a good voice, we would all sing together. It was just a great experience.

MAILER: What years were those? '46, '47?

CARTER: No, I would say later, '50, '51.

MAILER: I was there in the summer of '50.

CARTER: We may have been there at the same time.

September 26, 1976

We've Lost the Spirit in Our Nation

. . . We've lost the spirit in our nation. A spirit of youth, vigor, a spirit of confidence, self-reliance, a spirit of work and not of welfare, a spirit of caring for one another, a spirit of unity between the President and the Congress, between federal, state, and local levels of government, between government itself and our great private enterprise system, between labor, management, agriculture, science, education, industry. This has been lost, and that's not part of the consciousness or character of the American people. We've seen a loss of morality in domestic and foreign affairs. We've seen a forgetting about human rights, and we're ashamed of what our government is as we deal with other nations around the world, and that's got to be changed, and I'm going to change it.

The value of a working family's paycheck is less now than it was in 1968. The number of bankruptcies in small business is double what it was eight years ago. The average profits for business are down. The number of people on welfare has doubled. These kinds of statistics sound very bad in a debate or in a speech, but the devastating impact of them is on the businessman who went broke and on the person who had never before drawn a welfare check but now has to stand in line for food stamps. We've got an income tax structure that's a disgrace, it's got to be changed. And beginning next year, it's going to be changed.

The Democrats have always believed and have proven that we can have low inflation rates and low unemployment at the same time. The Republicans have demonstrated again and again, and particularly recently, that you can have high

196

unemployment and high inflation rates at the same time. That's the difference between the two parties, and that's why we're going to kick the Republicans out next January.

Poverty creates crime. A family who has to push an eighteen-year-old man or woman out of the home, maybe a law-abiding young person, because the welfare payments and the unemployment compensation, Social Security, doesn't apply to an eighteen-year-old, and when that young person wanders up and down the street for a week, two weeks, three weeks, without a chance for a job, there's a pushing toward shoplifting, breaking in automobiles, selling numbers rackets, prostitution, drugs. Poverty is not an excuse for crime. But it's a reason for or a cause of crime.

What this Republican administration has done to our country is not only devastating in economic terms, but is devastating in human terms. It has sapped away the aspects of our nation that have always made us proud. We have been disillusioned in recent years, in the aftermath of Vietnam, Cambodia, Chile, Pakistan, Angola, Watergate, CIA, FBI, Medicaid scandals. Those things have hurt us, and we need to do away with that kind of devastating blow to our country.

We now have no sense of unity. The American people want to get along with one another. There's no reason for us to be divided along racial lines or along sectional lines or partisan lines between government and private industry, between the President and the Congress, between black or white people, those who speak English, those who don't, those who've been here two years, those who've been here two hundred years. There's no reason for these divisions. We need to unify our nation. Not because of an absence of differences among us individually, but with a common purpose to correct our mistakes, to bind ourselves together, to ask the difficult questions, and to have once again a spirit that's endemic of our people and that's been absent in our government—

a spirit of hope and truth and compassion and love and brotherhood and competence for a change. That's got to come. It's going to come next year.

Rally
Portland, Oregon
September 27, 1976

Brotherhood and Sisterhood

In this speech, delivered to a coalition of women's groups, Carter gave a detailed statement of his position on women's issues. Near the end of the speech, encouraged by frequent applause, he departed from his text, and declared, among other things, that the American people are filled with a sense of brotherhood. Suddenly the cheers turned to jeers and cries of "Sisterhood, sisterhood." Carter quickly corrected himself, and for the rest of the campaign he generally spoke of "brotherhood and sisterhood."

First of all, let me say that I am pleased to be here and I am grateful to you for letting me come. I am very proud of what you are doing, completely in sympathy with you, wish you well, hope that you will be as tough and militant and as aggressive and as eloquent as you can humanly be, because the country is waiting for a strong voice from you, as a group. The country is waiting for adequate responses from political leaders who are listening to you. And I think not just in this country but other countries of the world. There is a great devastating discrimination against women throughout the globe. And unless we in our own country—whose lives are built around the Constitution, the Bill of Rights, equality of opportunity, individual liberty—unless we take the leadership, that leadership will be absent.

I'm grateful to come here as the only presidential candidate who addressed this group. I was proud to have been the first presidential candidate to endorse the Women's Agenda in its entirety, and I will be proud, beginning in January, to be the President who will implement your agenda. With your help, we'll do it.

The unfulfilled elements of the Women's Agenda are a terrible indictment of the Ford and Nixon administrations. Your demands and your legitimate aspirations have been blocked and circumvented by vetoes, indifference, and, on occasions of intense pressure from you, empty rhetoric.

We lack leadership in this country today. That's what this election is all about. And there are few areas where the absence of leadership is more dramatic than this administration's failure to work for equality of women. We need to restore the faith and the trust of our people in our own government. But we cannot expect America's women to have faith in a government that ignores your legitimate needs and aspirations and excludes you from the decision-making processes of your country's government. That must be changed.

If I become President, I'm determined to tear down the walls that have kept you out of the decision-making, policy-making participation in our government. And you can depend on that. I've long recognized the need for strong action to guarantee total equality of women in the areas of politics, education, employment, health care, housing, justice, and as one who comes from a family and a region where almost all the women work, at least in one job, I understand the special discrimination that has hurt women for so long in this country.

I particularly recognize the special economic forces that face women who work. My mother began working as a teenager, in a post office, and later as a registered nurse. And she's worked as a nurse until past her seventieth birthday, in this country and in India in the Peace Corps. My wife's father died when she was thirteen, and she began to work, washing hair in a beauty parlor and helping her mother, who was a seamstress. Rosalynn has always been a partner in our business. She is a full partner in our farm operation. And, as you know, we are equal partners in my political life.

I've seen this at first hand. In an area which has known discrimination in economic opportunity and is trying to overcome it, and in a part of the country that has known racial discrimination and is trying to overcome it, we are particularly conversant with the special aspects of economic deprivation, sex discrimination, that are still prevalent not just in one region but throughout the country. That must be changed in the future and without delay. The first step in providing economic equality for women is to ensure a stable national economy in which every person who wants to work can work. And in which the wage which is derived from that labor is not ravaged by quiet, undetected, insidious inflation. Furthermore, within the stable economy it's necessary to eliminate all forms of sexual discrimination, and to provide women for the first time in our history with economic opportunities equal to those of men.

Working women have been hardest hit by sexual discrimination, and by the inflation and unemployment that the Nixon and Ford administrations have inflicted on us all. I know who the last Americans are to be hired, I know who the first ones are to be discharged. I know who have the hardest time accommodating changes in income to meet rising inflationary pressure: the women of our country.

Let's look at the facts. Almost half of all families below the poverty line, and there are two and a half million more today than there were twelve months ago, are headed by women. And most of those are not satisfied with unemployment compensation or welfare. They are actively looking for jobs. Under the Republican administration the gap between wages paid to women who are working and wages paid to men who are working is increasing. Women now earn only fifty-eight percent as much as men for doing exactly the same work. We must understand too that, as bad as they are, these are not just dry statistics. These are men and women and children who are in need, who deserve national attention and leaders who will take action to help them. We do not have that leadership now. And we've not had it for eight long years. The policy of our government has been one of neglect.

Economic recovery will not come overnight. But there are several steps that as President I will take immediately to assist women who work.

First, I'm committed to join in developing a comprehensive child care program, which will help to fund state and local programs and provide subsidies or scaled fees for employed mothers in low- and moderate-income families. This will help restore the dignity of work to present welfare families and the right of gainful employment to all parents.

As you know, Richard Nixon vetoed comprehensive child care services. President Ford has equivocated on the issue, vetoed one bill, and signed another very weak bill, because it was an election year. I think all of you realize that Republican presidents have failed to realize that adequate child care services are just as essential to the children of mothers who work as food, shelter, and clothing.

I think you all know how hard my running mate, Senator Mondale, has worked for child care and other programs to strengthen the American family. I'm proud of him, he's my friend, we're partners, and we'll work together with you.

The second thing I want to mention is this. There are twenty-one federal agencies who now have responsibility for enforcing federal antidiscrimination regulations. But there is no coordination among them. Kennedy, Johnson, and the federal courts put on the lawbooks programs and commitments to eliminate discrimination. But the enforcement of these laws has been lax at best. On occasion, Nixon and Ford and their administrations have deliberately subverted or blocked implementation of those laws. I will work to assure that existing guidelines are strengthened and vigorously enforced, to ensure that women are hired, paid, and promoted on a basis of fairness and equality for a change.

The third point is this. Cases before the Equal Employment Opportunity Commission are hopelessly backlogged, literally for years, with thousands now awaiting settlement. With this delay, justice is blocked, because the original complaint or the witnesses who might have testified slowly dissipate in a rapidly changing mobile society. I will see that the EEOC staff is adequate to carry out its mandate, and I will also appoint additional women as EEOC commissioners. Presently, only one out of five members is female, a statistic that makes a travesty of the very purpose of an Equal Employment Opportunity Commission. We're going to change that very quickly when I become President.

Fourth, I would direct the Office of Federal Contract Compliance programs in the Department of Labor to enforce the executive order forbidding discrimination by federal contractors or subcontractors, so that women business owners can have a fair share of government contracts.

Fifth, women continue to be unrepresented in the federal government, especially in the supergrades, where you only hold three percent of the jobs. I will insist upon hiring policies that will bring far more women into the top grades, and throughout our government. This administration has only paid lip service to women's rights. It's been argued—always by men—that qualified women do not exist. They do exist. I intend to find them and put them to work.

The sixth point I want to make is this. Flexible hours and part-time work are an important point to the parents of school-age children who need additional income but just can't be gone from home eight or nine hours a day. They are also crucial to help retired people and some disabled people who are not physically able to work full time. Therefore, I want to encourage, actively and aggressively, the adoption in the federal government, and also use my influence in the private business sector, of flexible working times for men and women. And I will take action to increase the availability of part-time jobs, with proper provision for fringe benefits and for job security.

The seventh thing is this. I will act to curb unfair economic practices such as discrimination against women in obtaining credit and insurance. Businesswomen in particular have been held back by these unfair practices and they must be halted.

Eighth, I want to comment on a group that quite often is not mentioned, even among women's groups. I would actively support the American homemaker in every possible way.

The American homemaker is the foundation of the structure of our society. More women still work in their homes than outside their homes. But the rising divorce rate and early widowhood quite often leaves them highly vulnerable to economic deprivation and adversity. I will take action to help homemakers achieve equity in Social Security and divorce proceedings and tax laws and the probate of estates and to provide legal counseling to women who enter the job market for the first time, without the experience they need. This is the very least we can do, a small first step, to ease a painful transition that too many women must take each year.

Ninth, I will work toward equality in education. Education leads to self-sufficiency, and women must have equal access to it. Yet the statistics on financial aid tell that eighty percent of the nation's most prestigious fellowships and awards still go to men. Men dominate supervisory positions in our school systems, and still far outnumber women in our graduate schools. Inequity in federal financial aid to women will be eliminated during my administration.

In closing, let me say this. It's been a pleasure and an honor to be here. This is indeed a historic occasion, because since women's suffrage was finally granted, we've not had a nationwide coordinated commitment of different women's groups toward common purposes and goals. There have been few political developments in America in recent years that have impressed me more than the movement of women toward equal rights. In the face of opposition and misunderstanding you've gotten your message across to millions of women and to millions of men as well.

I've often said that the voting rights act was the best thing that ever happened to the South. It not only liberated blacks, but it liberated the whites as well. It permitted the South to move into the mainstream of American economic, political, and social life. In the same way I agree with you that the women's movement can do just as much for men as for women, by passing the Equal Rights Amendment. I hope that all of us can work together, myself as President, Fritz Mondale as Vice President, the members of our families and you, to induce those last four states to finally ratify the Equal Rights Amendment to give our women a chance in life.

I have to add that it's still not going to be easy. Because we haven't yet penetrated the consciousness of America with the patent, continuing discrimination against women. American people are fair. Once they can be convinced that women who work in factories and stores and businesses only get fifty-eight percent as much pay for the same labor, when they are convinced that women are the last ones hired and the first ones fired, when they are convinced that women's jobs are as important to them and their families as are the jobs of men, when we can convince the American people that discrimination against women now is just as severe and crippling to our national strength and consciousness as was religious or racial discrimination in the past, when we can convince the American people of those facts, then the legislatures will not be reluctant anymore and the John Birch Society will not prevail anymore, and we'll get ERA passed, and I believe we're going to do it.

Change doesn't come easily. My own campaign for President has not always been easy. It hasn't been an ordeal or a sacrifice for me. I've learned a lot about our great country. I've learned how to translate the impact of statistics into the impact on human lives. I've never had the support of powerful special-interest groups. In the primary nobody thought I had a chance to win. Some powerful political figures quite often supported my opponents. But my strength has been derived from within homes and factory shift lines and beauty parlors and barbershops and livestock sale barns and shopping centers. And that's where my strength still lies.

I have confidence in our country. I believe the average American is fair, and just wants to be treated fairly. I believe the average American is patriotic and still loves our country in spite of its past mistakes. I believe our country and its people are still idealistic, and filled with a sense of brotherhood and compassion and love.

Brotherhood and sisterhood.

I believe too that this is a nation that's looking for a chance to redeem itself from past mistakes, to answer difficult questions, to bind ourselves together in a common purpose. And as I said at the end of my acceptance speech, as brothers and sisters we can move into the future with confidence. I want to be sure that your effort is successful, that your agenda is met. I have, as you know, an eight-year-old daughter, Amy. I love her very much. I don't get to see her often. I hope when Amy becomes an adult that she can be just as sure of becoming a doctor as she can of being a nurse, that she can be just as sure of being a lawyer as she can a secretary. And that she can be just as sure of being President as a President's daughter.

> *Women's Agenda Conference*
> *Washington, D.C.*
> *October 2, 1976*

The Family Is the Cornerstone of American Life

EVER SINCE the founding days of Monsignor William Kerby, the National Conference of Catholic Charities has been a major force in maintaining diversity in the delivery of social services in America. But in recent years we've suffered in Washington a failure of leadership at the highest levels of our government. Instead of cooperation, your efforts have been met with indifference and negativism and neglect.

We saw a dramatic example of that negativism last week when the President vetoed the appropriations bill for the Departments of Labor, and Health, Education and Welfare, a veto that was wisely and very swiftly overridden by more than two-thirds of the members of both the House and Senate, including many members of the President's own party. Earlier we had seen vetoes of legislation to train and provide jobs for handicapped people. Vetoes of educational opportunities for Vietnam veterans. Vetoes of bills that would have provided two million jobs for Americans. Vetoes of bills that would have given training for licensed practical nurses.

If I become President, I intend to strengthen the American system of private volunteerism that is imperative if this nation is to meet its commitment for basic social justice. Pluralism in social services is of course only a part of a larger pluralism, ethnic, cultural, and religious, that has made America great and will keep America great. I've come more and more to appreciate the diversity and the greatness of our country since I have been a candidate for President. As you know, I'm a Baptist from the South. And you are Catholics from all parts of the country. Yet I'm convinced that the basic beliefs and the basic concerns that unite us, and none is more basic than freedom of religious expression, are far more important than the factors that divide us.

John Kennedy, speaking in 1960 to a meeting of ministers in Houston, said that while it was he a Catholic who faced suspicion that year, it would someday be, as he said, a Jew or a Baptist.

His prediction has come to pass. This year it is a Southern Baptist who faces the intense scrutiny that is so vital to our democratic process. I welcome the scrutiny. And I've not the slightest doubt that this year once again our national tradition of tolerance and fairness will prevail. As it did in 1928, when Georgia voted for Al Smith, as it did in 1960, when my State of Georgia gave John Kennedy an even greater percentage of its total vote than he got in his home state of Massachusetts.

I know that one of the common concerns that unites us is the preservation and the strengthening of the American family. It's a concern about which I've spoken many times during the campaign, and I would like to discuss this subject with you today.

The family is the cornerstone of American life. I'm deeply troubled by its deterioration in recent years, and by the fact that our elected leaders and our government agencies and programs have at times, through ignorance or indifference, pursued policies that have damaged families, rather than supporting and strengthening them.

If we want less government, and many of us do, then we must work for strong families. For when the family structure is weak, our government will tend to fill the vacuum, often unsatisfactorily.

The evidence of family breakdown is all around us. Two out of every five marriages now end in divorce. One child in eight is now born outside of marriage. One American child in six now lives in a single-parent family. A million young Americans run away from home every year. The second most

prevalent cause of death among young men fifteen to nineteen years old is suicide.

The problems are severe. The question is what our government is now going to do to lessen—or perhaps worsen—the
problem. The next question is what our government could
be doing if the proper leadership existed.

I don't apologize for a slightly partisan presentation. There
are some basic differences between the Republican Party and
the Democratic Party relating to your life's work and the
American family. I'm deeply concerned about the impact
that the Republican mismanagement of our economy is having on family life in America. The Republicans have given us
at the same time, and for the first time, both high inflation
and also high unemployment. The unemployment forces
people from work onto welfare and the inflation rate picks
the pockets of those working people who still are lucky
enough to have a job, or of older people who have some
semblance of income for their security.

Mr. Ford says he's proud of his economic record. And he's
running on it. He ought to be running from it. Is he proud
of the fact that two and a half million American families
slipped below the poverty level last year alone? Is he proud
of the fact that in the last two years we've added two and a
half million Americans to the unemployment rolls? In the
last three months, five hundred thousand more adult Americans became unemployed. Is he proud of the six percent
annual inflation rate that he and his advisers are trying to
convince us is normal for our great country?

I sometimes wonder how often the people who set economic policies for this administration stop to think of the
human realities that lie behind the unemployment and inflation statistics that they find so encouraging. Do they consider
what it is like for a man or a woman who can't provide for
their children, who may have been employed for fifteen or
twenty years and now find themselves standing for the first

time in a welfare line after a lifetime of honest and satisfying work? Are they aware of the mounting evidence that unemployment contributes greatly to increasing alcoholism, child abuse, drug addiction, mental illness, the divorce rate, juvenile delinquency, and even suicide?

In addition to its economic mismanagement, this administration has pursued policies that, through ignorance or indifference, have harmed families instead of helping families.

Let me give you a few examples. Welfare policies now in effect in more than half the states deny benefits unless and until the father leaves the home. Medicaid programs in twenty-one states actually deny prenatal care to first-time mothers, even though women who receive no prenatal care are three times as likely to have a child born with birth defects. Urban renewal policies have time after time destroyed neighborhoods and shattered families. Civil service regulations have provided little opportunity for flexible work schedules or for part-time employment that would help greatly a parent who must also take care of children.

Tax policies have discriminated against families in a variety of ways, such as the so-called grandmother clause, which for years has disallowed child-care tax deductions for family members if they are closer than a first cousin.

I've never seen a highway go through a golf course, but a lot of highways go through neighborhoods where two hundred family homes are destroyed.

I remember when the FHA was a hope for a family that wanted to own a home. But we've now seen monthly payments for homes more than doubled in the last eight years. The average family home now costs $46,000 and FHA last year lost six hundred million dollars because of inappropriate lending procedures. There were five hundred indictments in the Housing and Urban Development Department in recent years, and HUD has now become the world's worst slum landlord.

The examples go on and on, and the point is clear. Our government has often been blind to the need of American families. One thing I intend to do as President is to make sure that every action of government helps our families rather than hurts them. One step I'm going to take soon after becoming President is to call together with me a White House conference on the American family. My goal will be to bring together leaders of government, leaders of the private sector like yourselves, and just ordinary citizens and parents to discuss specific ways that we can better support and strengthen our families. That conference can be an important first step toward restoring the public and the private partnership that must exist if we are going to provide adequate social services to the American people.

Let me list for you briefly some of the programs that I will support as President which I believe will strengthen our families, our economy, and our society. First of all I support a comprehensive program of national health care.

I will also enact economic policies that will lower inflation, create jobs, and get our people off welfare and back to work again.

I intend to reform our present welfare system. About ten percent of our people who are chronically on welfare are able to work full time. There is nothing wrong with them physically or mentally; they're not old, they're not blind. They should be removed from the welfare system altogether, placed under the responsibility of the Labor Department, the Education Department, given job training, literacy instruction if they can't read and write, the services of public and private job placement agencies, and matched with a job. If they are offered a job and they don't take it, I would not pay them any more benefits.

The other ninety percent cannot work full time. We ought to treat them with love and compassion and concern. We ought to have a fairly uniform nationwide payment to meet the basic necessities of life.

I believe that from out of our national diversity can come national unity—if the people rule again.

I believe that we have lived through a time of torment, and now we are near a time of healing—if the people rule again.

I ask you to help us reach that point of healing, to help us bind up our nation's wounds. I can think of no more fitting words to close than those of your own Monsignor John O'Grady, who said, "The Magna Carta of Catholic charity was written on Mount Olivet when Jesus Christ said to his disciples, 'For I was hungry, and you gave me to eat, I was thirsty and you gave me to drink, I was stranger and you took me in, I was in prison and you came to me. I say to you, as long as you did it to one of these, my brethren, you did it to me.'"

That is the spirit that has made the Catholic Charities great. It is a spirit that can restore our nation's greatness. It is the spirit in which I come before you today. I ask you for your help. You can count on mine.

The National Conference of Catholic Charities
Denver, Colorado
October 4, 1976

The Second Carter–Ford Debate: Foreign Policy

QUESTION: . . . Do you really have a quarrel with the Republican record? Would you not have done any of those things? CARTER: Well I think the Republican administration has been almost all style and spectacular and not substance. We've got a chance tonight to talk about, first of all, leadership, the character of our country and a vision of the future. In every one of these instances, the Ford administration has failed, and I hope tonight that I and Mr. Ford will have a chance to discuss the reasons for those failures.

Our country is not strong anymore; we're not respected anymore. We can only be strong overseas if we're strong at home, and when I become President we will not only be strong in those areas but also in defense—a defense capability second to none.

We've lost in our foreign policy the character of the American people. We've ignored or excluded the American people and the Congress from participation in the shaping of our foreign policy. It's been one of secrecy and exclusion. In addition to that we've had a chance to become now—contrary to our longstanding beliefs and principles—the arms merchant of the whole world. We've tried to buy success from our enemies, and at the same time we've excluded from the process the normal friendship of our allies.

In addition to that we've become fearful to compete with the Soviet Union on an equal basis. We talk about détente. The Soviet Union knows what they want in détente, and they've been getting it. We have not known what we wanted, and we've been out-traded in almost every instance.

The other point I want to make is about our defense.

We've got to be a nation blessed with a defense capability that is efficient, tough, capable, well organized. Narrowly focused fighting capabilities, the ability to fight, if necessary, is the best way to avoid a chance for or the requirement to fight.

And the last point I want to make is this: Mr. Ford and Mr. Kissinger have continued on with the policies and pledges of Richard Nixon. Even the Republican platform has criticized the lack of leadership in Mr. Ford and they've criticized the foreign policy of this administration. This is one instance where I agree with the Republican platform.

I might say this in closing, and that is that as far as foreign policy goes, Mr. Kissinger has been the President of this country. Mr. Ford has shown an absence of leadership, and an absence of a grasp of what this country is and what it ought to be. That's got to be changed. And that's one of the major issues in this campaign of 1976.

FORD: . . . If we turn to Helsinki—I'm glad you raised it, Mr. Frankel. In the case of Helsinki, thirty-five nations signed an agreement, including the Secretary of State for the Vatican. I can't under any circumstances believe that the—His Holiness, the Pope—would agree by signing that agreement that the thirty-five nations have turned over to the Warsaw Pact nations the domination of Eastern Europe. It just isn't true. And if Mr. Carter alleges that His Holiness by signing that has done that, he is totally inaccurate.

And what has been accomplished by the Helsinki agreement? Number one, we have an agreement where they notify us and we notify them of any military maneuvers that are to be undertaken. They have done it. . . . There is no Soviet domination of Eastern Europe and there never will be under a Ford administration.

QUESTION: . . . I'm sorry, did I understand you to say, sir, that the Russians are not using Eastern Europe as their own sphere of influence in occupying most of the countries there and making sure with their troops that it's a communist zone, whereas on our side of the line the Italians and the French are still flirting with . . .

FORD: I don't believe, Mr. Frankel, that the Yugoslavians consider themselves dominated by the Soviet Union. I don't believe that the Rumanians consider themselves dominated by the Soviet Union. I don't believe that the Poles consider themselves dominated by the Soviet Union.

Each of those countries is independent, autonomous, it has its own territorial integrity and the United States does not concede that those countries are under the domination of the Soviet Union. As a matter of fact, I visited Poland, Yugoslavia, and Rumania to make certain that the people of those countries understood that the President of the United States and the people of the United States are dedicated to their independence, their autonomy, and their freedom.

MODERATOR: Governor Carter, now if you will respond.

CARTER: Well in the first place, I'm not criticizing His Holiness, the Pope. I was talking about Mr. Ford.

The fact is that secrecy has surrounded the decisions made by the Ford administration. In the case of the Helsinki agreement, it may have been a good agreement at the beginning, but we have failed to enforce the so-called basket-three part, which insures the right of people to migrate, to join their families, to be free, to speak out. The Soviet Union is still jamming Radio Free Europe. . . .

We've also seen a very serious problem with the so-called Sonnenfeldt document—which apparently Mr. Ford has just endorsed—which said that there's an organic linkage between the Eastern European countries and the Soviet Union. I would like to see Mr. Ford convince the Polish-Americans and the Czech-Americans and the Hungarian-Americans in this country that those countries don't live under the domination and supervision of the Soviet Union behind the Iron Curtain.

San Francisco, California
October 6, 1976

Warm Hearts and Cool Heads

... I WAS told that I'm the first Southerner to come and speak to your annual banquet. I hope that I won't be the last Southerner to come here. We've had in our country too much of stereotypes, and if I do become President, one of the things I hope to accomplish will be to break down many of the old stereotypes about liberals and conservatives that have been in the path of progress, and have discouraged serious political discourse throughout the country for too many years.

In domestic affairs, too many conservative stereotypes have portrayed liberals as fuzzy-headed and wasteful, and the conservatives on the other hand as realistic and efficient. And liberals sometimes see themselves as overflowing with the compassion that the hardhearted conservatives always lack.

I reject both stereotypes. And I must say that in the past eight years we have seen that good solid Republican ideologues can be just as wasteful and incompetent and fuzzy-headed as anyone who has ever lived. That's been too much demonstrated, it's got to be changed next January.

The stereotypes bear little resemblance to the real world, in which we find a lot of people who combine both compassion and competence, who have, in Adlai Stevenson's phrase, both warm hearts and cool heads. These are the kinds of people that you'll be seeing in the Carter administration next year.

Also, our national foreign policy dialogue has been too often distorted by clichés and polarization. The code words in foreign policy have been "soft" and "tough." We've suffered enough in this country because some presidents and their advisers have felt it necessary to prove their supposed "toughness" by pursuing rash and ultimately tragic policies. It's time for our foreign policy to concern itself with real wisdom rather than imagined toughness.

A strong nation, like a strong person, can afford to be gentle, firm, thoughtful, and restrained. It can afford to extend a helping hand to others. It's a weak nation, like a weak person, that must behave with bluster and boasting and rashness and other signs of insecurity. . . .

We've lost a lot in this country in the last eight years. We've lost some precious things that we've believed in in the past, that we took for granted. We've lost trust in our government.

But I don't think it has to be that way. I think that what happened in the last eight years has been a temporary aberration. I think we were tricked and misled in many instances. Now we are a wiser and a more skeptical nation, and I welcome that skepticism. I welcome the scrutiny of our people. I'm not going to hide in a Rose Garden. I'm going to be out campaigning every minute that I can from now until the election, because the campaign itself is a tremendous educational opportunity. To travel around this nation, to meet American people, to talk a little, to listen a lot, to receive questions and suggestions and expressions of the hopes and dreams of 215 million of us is sobering, sometimes it's humbling, most of the time inspirational, always educational.

We went through a series of primaries, thirty primaries. And I learned a lot about this country. I learned that it is still strong. Economically, we're the strongest nation on earth. God's blessed us with broad fields, that have now become almost the breadbasket of the world. And powerful, pure streams and pure air and access to the oceans, and tremendous mineral deposits. That strength has not been changed.

We still have the best system of government on earth. Richard Nixon didn't hurt it. Watergate didn't hurt it. The

CIA revelations, the wars in Vietnam and Cambodia didn't hurt our system of government. It's still clean and decent. It's a basis on which we can predicate answers to complicated questions, and bind ourselves together and correct our mistakes and approach the future with confidence in one another. But the greatest resource of all is the 215 million Americans who have within us the same strength and character and idealism and patriotism and confidence and eagerness to work for the good of one another that's always made our country strong.

But our nation has been in trouble the last eight years. I think we agree that the country needs new leadership if it is once again to achieve its tremendous potential. The world needs a great America. You and I want a great America. If you give me your help, then once again I'm sure that we will have a great America.

Liberal Party Dinner
New York, New York
October 14, 1976

Crime Is Unacceptable

THE TIME has come to declare that crime is unacceptable in our nation and to harness the combined resources of all government agencies and private efforts to achieve an orderly society.

The purpose of our system of law is to ensure justice. But first it must permit our people to be safe in our homes, on our streets, and in our places of business, meeting, and worship.

Eight years ago Mr. Nixon ran for President on a platform of law and order. He promised he would wage a war against crime.

He did not keep that promise. In eight years of Republican rule, serious crimes have gone up by fifty-eight percent, and twenty-seven percent in the last two years alone.

We must remember that crime and lack of justice are especially cruel to those least able to protect themselves.

Restoring order to our society is not a question of liberal versus conservative, Republican versus Democrat, black versus white, rich versus poor.

It is a question of leadership.

Recently we saw another example of the failure of leadership in this Republican administration. Two weeks ago Mr. Ford promised that he would start a hundred-day war against crime next January if he is elected for another term.

Mr. Ford has already been in office for eight hundred days. There are a hundred days left before January twentieth, 1977.

He has no plan. If he wants to reduce crime, why doesn't he start his crusade now?

The Republicans have also tragically set an example not of respect for the law, but of violation of the law.

The Attorney General of the United States should be the highest symbol of honest, impartial administration of the law. But two Republican Attorneys General in the last eight years have been convicted of serious criminal acts.

The FBI has been shaken and demoralized by accusations of illegal conduct, and by efforts by the White House to use the FBI for political ends.

The Drug Enforcement Agency, created in 1973, has already been tainted by scandals that forced its director to resign.

Our overcrowded court system is now a major cause of crime. Career criminals take advantage of the system, often committing additional crimes and terrorizing potential witnesses while out on bail.

We should encourage local police to give priority to violent crimes—assault, robbery, rape, muggings, murders. When I was Governor of Georgia, we stopped treating alcoholism as a crime to provide increased medical help to alcoholics and to free our police and courts to concentrate on violent crimes.

I visited Georgia's prisons many times, and almost all the inmates I met there were poor. Poor people aren't the only ones to commit crimes, but they seem to be the only ones who go to prison.

The corporate criminal, the middle-class criminal, the white-collar criminal, too often get off with a slap on the wrist.

This can only cause contempt for the whole concept of equal justice.

White-collar crimes cost this country at least forty billion dollars a year. Yet there has not been a single felony indictment for price-fixing since Mr. Ford took office.

Every time a person goes back to prison as a repeat offender, it is a sign that our prisons have failed. I believe we can reduce the percentage of failures and at the same time reduce the amount of crime.

Presidential leadership can make a difference.

We can make our existing crime-fighting programs more efficient and effective.

We can have a stronger economy, and more jobs for our people, and that will lessen crime.

I think our country's leaders, beginning with the President, can set an example and set a tone that will increase respect for the law and increase the sense of national unity, and that can lessen crime in America.

Crime reflects sickness in a society.

I think that, working together, we can make ours a more healthy society, and one in which we need not live our lives in fear. I intend, as President, to provide the leadership that will turn the tide against the scourge of crime.

I ask your help in that great undertaking.

City Club
Detroit, Michigan
October 15, 1976

We Don't Know God's Purpose on Earth

U.S. Representative Jerry Litton of Missouri died along with his wife, Sharon, and their two children, Scott and Linda, in a private plane crash on the night of August 3, 1976. Only hours before, Litton had won the Democratic nomination for the U.S. Senate race that fall. Carter had met Litton once, was greatly impressed with him, and agreed to address a memorial dinner for the Litton family on October 15. Earlier in the day he delivered his crime speech in Detroit, and he had only about two hours to prepare his remarks for the dinner, which he delivered from notes.

MORE THAN a year ago, when I was beginning my own campaign for the nomination for President of the United States, I came here at the invitation of Congressman Jerry Litton to participate one Sunday in what was one of the most remarkable experiences of my life—Dialogues with Litton. I never dreamed what it would be. But I was looking for exposure and I was looking for experience—learning about politics—and I came. I could not believe that a thousand people would pay a fee to come together on a Sunday afternoon to ask questions of a Congressman.

It was an unbelievable interrelationship between him and the people who sat around a tremendous ballroom and asked question after question after question to him and to me. To have it recorded on tape and later played back to viewers who had grown up in several states who had perhaps their first opportunity to see tough cross-examination given to those who actually represent them in government—there was an intimacy about it that was startling.

I thought a lot about that meeting when I went back home to Plains, Georgia. How we often draw away from people who have trust in us once we get in office. But Jerry Litton had, with a great sensitivity, figured out a unique way to stay close to folks back home. He let them feel not that he was reaching down to them or telling them about distant happenings in Washington but that they were part of it and they were helping him make the decisions. It was a very great experience.

When I got back home I told my wife, Rosalynn, "I have just met a young man who shocked me and who startled me and who inspired me. And I believe that someday he has a good chance to be President of the United States. Because there is something about him that's unique." I never had known him before.

As soon as I made my official announcement as a candidate for President, Jerry Litton endorsed me. Now, I don't criticize the rest of the Missouri delegation when I say that he was the first one who did. And we had only had a brief encounter, relatively speaking, but there was a kind of mutuality about it, of friendship and trust. And it's a compliment to me that that spirit was built up between us.

Jerry Litton was blessed by his family, as you well know. His mother and father, and his wife and children, they were a team. And I know the benefit in that. Because a lot of times in politics, as you well know, it's a lonely thing. Particularly when you are just getting started—running for Congress or running for Governor or running for President.

Most of the time, in those early stages, when you say, "I want to be Congressman of the Sixth District," and then you walk away, you know there are a lot of jokes and smirking, and you feel very humble. To walk in front of a service station and talk to five people and say, "Would you vote for me for Congress?" And quite often you feel that you are not quite worthy in their eyes. You think more of yourself, but you're sure that they don't think you're qualified to go to Washington.

But the family that's there—your wife and others who have confidence in you—always provide a base, a solid base, that's unshakable. And you can take the ups and downs, endorsements and endorsements of your opponents, favorable newspaper editorials and those that are very critical, success in a speech and a speech that fumbles. And with the bad editorials, and the endosements for your opponent, and the speeches that fail, it's always great to come home to a wife who is an equal partner in the process.

Jerry Litton and his family—three generations at least—provide an inspiration to us, and an inspiration to him. He was born, like I was, on an isolated farm—before the Roosevelt-Truman era—without electricity, without indoor plumbing. But it didn't hurt us. And he became at a very early age a young man who made the best of his opportunities. There was not a handicap or an obstacle that caused him to be discouraged or to withdraw from the competition of an increasingly adult world. He went to high school, he was president of a national honor society. He joined the FFA, as I did as a high school boy. And he not only succeeded at his own high school—I was secretary of the Plains High School FFA—but he went on beyond that and became the president of all the Future Farmers of Missouri. And he wasn't satisfied with that. He went on and became a national officer.

He began to make speeches when he was young. Because he was so timid, and he saw that as a potential obstacle as he grew up, he took lessons within the Future Farmers to learn how to speak. He would go and make speeches at graduation exercises, and travel around the country and by the time he got to college he had accumulated fifteen thousand dollars to help his family pay his way through school with his speaking ability. His common subject was farmers and agriculture and rural life and the commonality of purpose and challenge and opportunity between those who live in the great cities of our country and those who live in the great farmland of our country.

His father had a great deal of bad luck, injured as a truck driver, laid up, almost completely physically incapacitated for seven years, and later hurt again, so when Jerry came home from college he had the great responsibility of a small farm. And he and his father formed a partnership that existed throughout the rest of his life.

He did not set as a goal for himself of having a mediocre or an average ranch operation. He knew about a new breed of cattle, the French Charolais, and he told his father, "Let's buy the best," and they bought the best they could afford. But he still wasn't satisfied. And in those embryonic days, with the use of computers, they analyzed the qualities of every calf and every brood cow and every bull, and they slowly improved upon a superlative breed of cattle, until, in just a few years, starting from practically nothing, with a twenty-thousand-dollar loan, he and his father, working together with the rest of their family, built up a cattle herd that was known throughout the world.

And then Jerry decided he wanted to go to Congress. In fact he decided when he was nineteen years old that he wanted to go to Congress when he was thirty-five. So guess what happened? When he was thirty-five years old, he was elected to Congress. And because he wanted to avoid any conflict of interest, he decided to sell his interest in the ranch. It was worth a little more than twenty thousand dollars—in fact a little more than three and a half million dollars. But he severed his conflict in the business world and gave his life to the people he represented in government.

He went to Congress as a freshman. He started the kind of career that he had spelled out at an early date, when as a FFA officer he visited my favorite President, Harry Truman. He went there with a fifteen-minute appointment and he stayed two hours. They talked about the greatness of this country and the need for unity and the obstacles that could be overcome.

Jerry Litton told Harry Truman about his future desire to be in government. And Harry Truman said, "Well, you can go one of two ways. You can go through the courthouse, start at the lower level, work your way up, become part of the political establishment. Or you can go into business and launch your career based on a direct non-political interrelationship with voters." When Jerry Litton got to Congress, he had taken Truman's second piece of advice, and he had a direct, unrestrained interrelationship with the voters who sent him there.

In his first election he won a tough battle against several opponents—five or six—with an overwhelming victory. In 1974 he ran for re-election and won with seventy-nine percent of the vote. In the whole history of the district, the highest that anyone had ever gotten before was sixty-four percent.

Jerry Litton got to the Congress, and he made it very clear to everyone at first that he would not take orders from anyone in the congressional structure. Tip O'Neill, who is very likely to be the next Speaker of the House, commented on Jerry Litton while he was still a freshman. He said, "I've been in the Congress twenty-two years and I have never yet met a freshman member of Congress who could equal Jerry Litton."

I think you see clearly that Jerry Litton's successes were not accidents. He owed his success to his friends who had confidence in him. He never betrayed that confidence, or the commitment to principles that never changed. He owed his success to a great exuberance. He didn't trudge through life, plodding one step at a time. He ran through life with a great happiness and a joy. He never let a potential obstacle deter him. In fact, sometimes I think he welcomed it. The tough battles, the uphill fights, challenged him and let him draw on the strength that came from the support of his family and friends.

That is the kind of politics that ought to exist more often in our country. Tonight we come to pay tribute to him. I'm saddened by it. I called his parents as soon as I heard about the tragedy. But tonight is not a time of sorrow. We've been through that sorrowful period. God's blessed us by having had a chance to know Jerry Litton. Or to know about him. And I hope that the few remarks that I've made tonight will impress on each one of us, including myself, some of those unchanging characteristics of human potential that should inspire us all. To be a little better. To set a slightly higher standard in our own lives. Not to be satisfied with mediocrity, but excellence. Not to be concerned only about the problems of our country, but to recognize its present and potential greatness.

He was deeply concerned about one aspect of politics which prevails now perhaps. He got there, as you know, in the midst of Watergate. And one of the last comments that Jerry Litton made was that the most devastating result of Watergate was the disillusionment of the American people, particularly young people, about our own government.

Well, Jerry Litton knows, I know, you know, that the American government is still clean and decent. It hasn't been damaged, the system hasn't. The problem has not been that the American people don't trust our leaders. The problem has been that some of our leaders haven't trusted the American people. But there has to be a mutuality of trust in order for us to derive the greatest strength in our own lives individually, and our own lives collectively—as we make up the United States of America. Because we, collectively, are what our nation is.

Jerry Litton saw that, I believe, as a farm boy at Chillicothe High School and at the University of Missouri and on the ranch and in the Congress. And he decided to run for the Senate, as you know. And the night the tragedy occurred he was the nominee of the Democratic Party for the United States Senate.

Well, we don't ever know what causes tragedies, or what God's purpose is on earth. But we do know that our own life here is transient. All of us. But what we leave behind is important. And although Jerry Litton may not have his own family here to carry on in generations to come, he has us and other people who knew him, who can maybe extract something, large or small, from him, and let it be part of our own lives to pass on from one year to another.

It's hard for me to pick out some written phrase that might be appropriate. I have to admit that I had several suggestions from people who said, "Read this, this is what Jerry Litton meant to me." But one of the people who worked with Jerry Litton thought that Shakespeare would be the best source—you've heard this repeated before. I'm going to take some poetic license and express it in the plural and let it apply to Jerry Litton and his whole family. This is from Shakespeare:

> When they shall die
> Take them and cut them out in little stars
> And they shall make the heavens so fine
> That all the world will be in love with night.

Jerry Litton Memorial Dinner
Kansas City, Missouri
October 15, 1976

Our Technology Has Outstripped Our Humanity

I WAS raised by a nurse. My mother this year is seventy-eight years old. She has devoted her life to caring for other people. Nothing would please her better than to be here with you today. However, it happens to be Amy's birthday, and this takes precedence, I'm afraid, even over professional enjoyment.

I'm thankful to come and make a statement, as the prospective President of our country, about a subject that is so important to me and to you and to 215 million other Americans.

There is a great deal of concern and confusion in our country about what ought to be done about health care. Sometimes when you have the best intentions and really want to fulfill commitments and ideas and ideals, there's a great deal of confusion about what needs to be done. And that's the case in our nation right now as we, the greatest nation on earth, struggle with the problem of how to let our own country provide healthy bodies and minds for our people.

We have excellent medical care for the very few who can afford it and who are educated enough to get doctors' advice in advance. But we have an inadequate health care program for those who are not well educated and for those who cannot afford expensive care. In short, there is a tragic gap between what our national health should be and could be, and what it now is.

Our technology in many instances has outstripped our basic humanity. Sophisticated and costly medical technology has improved our health, but its duplication and misutilization have wasted our nation's wealth. And the scarcity of financial and human resources then restrains the budget for

229

other health and social needs. It's time for us to get back to the basics, and the basic need of any health care system is to care about people and to prevent disease and injury before they happen.

Prevention is both cheaper and simpler than cure. But we have stressed the latter—cure—and we have ignored to an increasing degree the former—prevention. Our traditional self-reliance, our emphasis on family and community health, our concern about the prevention of disease, regular check-ups, early diagnosis, and early treatment has almost been forgotten by many in the onrush of technology and increasing specialization. In recent years, we've spent forty cents out of every health dollar on hospitalization. In effect, we've made the hospital the first line of defense, instead of the last. By contrast, we only spend three cents on disease prevention and control, less than half a cent on health education, and a quarter of a cent on environmental health.

I grew up in an isolated community in Georgia. We didn't have electricity, we didn't have running water. But I had adequate access to public and private health care—not just from my mother. But the major interrelationships I had with doctors and nurses was to prevent disease. And those of you in the audience who are as old as I am remember the threat of almost sure death from many of those horrible diseases, like diphtheria, cholera, polio, mumps, measles, whooping cough, typhus, and typhoid. The emphasis on health care in my life was not to wait until after I got sick, but to prevent my getting sick. That emphasis in the last forty years has been lost.

It needs to be restored.

A vast amount of our ill health is caused by the way we live, by the environment we've created, and by the lifestyles we've adopted. It is not the role of government to dictate lifestyles. But it is the proper role of government to educate our citizens and to aggressively stress the promotion of good health.

The biggest killer of our young people is not a disease but accidents, mainly automobile accidents. It should not be beyond the capacity of a concerned society to reduce those needless deaths and maimings. Among young men fifteen to twenty years old today the second most frequent cause of death is suicide. This is a shocking fact.

The major killer of middle-aged men is heart disease, often brought on by overeating and smoking and a lack of exercise and a lack of knowledge. It should not be beyond the capacity of a concerned society to reduce those unnecessary deaths.

The fact is, if we were to improve our national eating and drinking and smoking and exercise habits, we could be healthier, be happier, live longer, and save ourselves billions of dollars in the process.

I think presidential leadership and the tapping of the tremendous resources assembled in this ballroom could lead us toward a reduction in these unnecessary deaths.

We must be concerned too about environmental and occupational health threats. Environmental factors such as smoking, synthetic compounds in our food and water, exposure to industrial and commercial chemicals and air pollution, now cause an estimated seventy to ninety percent of all cancer. We've discovered cancer "hot spots," where industrial pollution causes dramatically high cancer rates. Yet for eight years this Republican administration has failed to enforce legislation and has opposed new legislation that would reduce the pollution that is killing our people. That's a failure of leadership again, and it must be stopped.

Let me outline for you some of the goals of the next administration in the area of health.

- We must have a comprehensive program of national health insurance.
- We must stress health and nutrition education. Our public schools could do more to teach our young people the dangers of drinking, smoking, using

drugs, overeating, and eating the wrong kinds of food.

- We must mount a renewed attack on cancer and other diseases caused by toxic chemicals in the environment, including strict enforcement of the new Toxic Substances Control Act.
- We must continue and expand biomedical research and be sure that it serves the health needs of all our people.
- We must have—and I intend to provide—government reorganization that will end the bureaucratic fragmentation that now frustrates any hope for a rational and effective national health policy. This is crucial—it must be done.
- We must encourage, and you can certainly help with this, alternative delivery systems such as health maintenance organizations and rural group practices. We must also remember that it's both more cost-efficient and more health-effective to use less expensive treatment methods where possible, to improve outpatient services instead of overbuilding and overusing hospitals.

  I think that the cooperation of insurance companies, hospitals, nursing homes, doctors, nurses, and patients' families to hold down the cost of what care there is, and to give adequate health care without wasting our scarce resources, is a great opportunity for the future.
- We must clean up the disgraceful Medicaid scandals. That is important, that must be done, and it will be done.
- We must encourage nursing home standards of safety, sanitation, and care, and we must encourage programs that will serve elderly people in their own homes whenever possible.

- Finally, we must, by scholarships, by loans, and by other means, provide medical education to more students, for minority and low-income families and also to more women, and we must encourage young health professionals to train and practice in rural and inner city areas.

In some countries there has been a dramatic recent shift toward women becoming medical doctors. This really ought to be done in our own country. And I'll do all I can to help with that.

These are some of the goals in the health field that I will work toward if I'm elected President. I don't claim to know all the answers. I do know that good health ought to be a right and not just a luxury, and that good government has no more responsibility and solemn and deep concern than to make possible good health for all its people.

American Public Health Association
Miami Beach, Florida
October 19, 1976

Give Our System Another Chance

... WE FACE a clear-cut choice this year between the past and the future, between more of the same and a new beginning. The Republicans have no new ideas, they don't even pretend to. All they can say is, in effect, "It can't be any better, so why worry about the election? Why worry about the government?" And they imply that somehow or another we ought to fear progress, or fear the future. But Americans have never feared progress and we've never feared the future. The American dream is based on a belief that with hard work and good government we can build better lives and build a better nation for ourselves and for our children. More of the same economic problems that we've experienced means more unemployment. It means additional human suffering.

People like us don't suffer nearly as much as the ones to whom I talked in Harlem this afternoon. And in Winston-Salem this afternoon. And in Miami this morning. And last night in Tampa. They come, having suffered when the unemployment rolls increase, because their families stand in line looking for a job. They come, having suffered when the unemployment rate rises, because they have to cut into their own personal expenses—food, clothing, housing. Most of us don't. And they come, having suffered with a loss of a commitment to a nation and ideals and principles that have been damaged very seriously in the last eight years.

The Republicans have had eight years to solve the problems of this nation, but they failed. I don't doubt that they tried. They've employed economic policies in which they believe. Their methods just didn't work. They didn't work under Herbert Hoover, they didn't work under Richard Nixon, and they're not working under Gerald Ford.

By every measure of growth and stability and progress and the quality of life, our society is now worse than it was when Lyndon Johnson left the White House and Richard Nixon and Gerald Ford moved in. Yet all they offer us is more of the same. Their intentions may be good, I don't doubt that. But we can't settle for good intentions while the people of our country are out of work and inflation continues to climb, and our nation's economy grinds to a halt.

We got the results today of an analysis of the gross national product. It's dropped more than half since January. We just can't stand four more years of stagnation. Our nation is crying out for leadership; our nation is crying out for a concept of greatness.

A great nation can't stand still. If we're not moving forward, we're moving backward. Our nation has always been at its best when as a people we were boldly reaching out, striving, trying, growing, facing difficulties with courage, with a spirit of unity, and the concept of excellence. And sometimes sacrifice.

I think of the Civilian Conservation Corps that I knew about when I was a child on the farm. I was too young to participate, but my first cousins did. I think about the REA when it turned on the electric lights in my house when I was fourteen years old. I think about the Marshall Plan under Truman and aid to Turkey and Greece and the United Nations and the formation of the nation of Israel. I think about the Peace Corps in which my mother served when she was about seventy years old.

But we don't have those concepts anymore. Of sacrifice and a struggle upward and inspiration and pride. We've had eight long tragic years, we've been stalled too long. We've got to get moving again, and only a new and fresh and vigorous and imaginative and dedicated Democratic leadership is going to get us moving. Not just in the White House but throughout the ranks of the federal, state, and local levels of government. And among people who hunger for something clean and decent around which they can build their lives once again.

The problem isn't just economic, it's a matter of the spirit. We as a nation have been disillusioned, we've suffered too much, and in too short a time. The assassination of great political leaders—John Kennedy, Bobby Kennedy, Martin Luther King, Jr.—a tragic war, hidden deceitfully from the American people in the case of Cambodia. A national scandal, the resignation and disgrace of a President of the United States, and the Vice President of the United States.

All of these things and others made millions of American people lose faith and trust in our own government. To all of these people I say every day, many times, please, don't give up. Don't be apathetic. Give our system another chance. To those who are disgusted or filled with apathy I say our government can work, and it will work, if we can only have leaders once again who have wisdom, and who are as good in office as the people who put them in office. That's what this campaign is all about. We must have a government that listens to our people and understands our people and respects our people and reflects the greatness of our people.

Government by the people. It's as simple as that. But our government in recent years has lost touch with our people, has become the servant of the few and not the many. That's what we must change, whether we are rich and powerful or poor and insecure. Whether we are socially prominent or not. I don't know all the answers. I'm just like you are. But I haven't given up hope for our country.

Democratic Party Dinner
New York, New York
October 19, 1976

A Child of the City

AL SMITH was a child of the city. The Lower East Side was his kindergarten. He once told a Cornell man that his alma mater was FFM—the Fulton Fish Market. He was a child of the city who became, in the words of one biographer, the hero of all cities.

He understood the strengths and the complexities of our great cities. He loved their people. He fought for their interests. We must be committed to that same difficult fight. We must say to New York City not "Drop dead" but "Stay alive, hang on, help is on the way, together we'll live forever."

Al Smith was a man with a passion for social justice. He knew instinctively that, as I said in my acceptance speech in Madison Square Garden, love must be aggressively translated into simple justice.

Throughout a long career in politics Al Smith applied his great charm and intelligence and his leadership abilities to the task of translating his moral convictions into social realities. That's not always easy. That effort is not always trusted by outside observers. But he was successful. He sponsored legislation to require factories to limit their working hours for men and women and little children, to reform workmen's compensation laws, to bring women into government, and to reform the civil service. He did a lot of innovative things in political years gone by. His enemies called him a socialist, but in truth he was a great humanist, a great reformer, a great prophet of the better America that was to come.

I think everyone here will agree that Al Smith would have made a great President. But he was denied that office, and we were denied his service, partially because of religious prejudice. Down in my state, Georgia, despite a campaign of smear and fear, Al Smith received 56.6 percent of the votes—more than he got in his home state of New York. We've always been proud of that vote.

But Al Smith lost the election and it was not until 1960 that another Catholic ran for President. John Kennedy also faced religious prejudice. But he was able to triumph over it. He was helped, I might add again, by my state of Georgia, which gave him 62.5 percent of its vote, more even than his home state of Massachusetts.

So our country is overcoming its prejudices and its stereotypes of the past. We are of course a nation of differences. Those differences don't make us weak. They're the source of our strength. Some of us too often forget that fact. The question is not when we came here—two years ago, twenty years ago, two hundred years ago—but why our families came here. And what we did after we arrived.

Our nation has sometimes been called a melting pot, but that's not an accurate description, because when our families come to this country, we've not been trying to give up our individuality, our uniqueness. We are proud of our differences. I think of our country more as a mosaic, built up of small component parts that are different from one another, sometimes individually not very beautiful, but when put together, we make a picture of liberty and freedom and equality of opportunity that is unique in the history of all humankind.

Al Smith represented one group in the beautiful mosaic of America, a group with a love of literature and poetry, a love of life, a love of family, a love of country, a love of freedom, and a love of God.

H. L. Mencken wrote of Al Smith, "Somewhere in the sidewalks of New York he picked up the doctrine that it is better to be honest than to lie. It's not a popular doctrine in America," said Mencken. "It is dangerous baggage for politics.

But it has merit, nevertheless," he said. "It makes a man comfortable inside."

I feel very comfortable tonight talking about Al Smith in your presence, being with you, and associating myself with the great tradition, along with all those who are interested in politics in our country, of the great man whom we honor.

If I should become President, I intend to fight for the same principles for which he fought so long and so hard, along with you, because I know and you know that he and many others before us have done it with such rare and brilliant distinction. That's what's made our country great.

Al Smith Dinner
New York, New York
October 21, 1976

Closing Statement, Third Carter–Ford Debate

THE MAJOR purpose of an election for President is to choose a leader—someone who can analyze the depth of feeling in our country, to set a standard for our people to follow, to inspire people to reach for greatness, to correct our defects, to answer difficult questions, to bind ourselves together in a spirit of unity.

I don't believe the present administration has done that. We have been discouraged and we've been alienated. Sometimes we've been embarrassed. Sometimes we've been ashamed that people are out of work and there's a sense of withdrawal. But our country is innately very strong.

Mr. Ford is a good and decent man, but he's been in office now more than eight hundred days, approaching almost as long as John Kennedy was in office. I'd like to ask the American people what's been accomplished. A lot remains to be done.

My own background is different from his. I was a school board member and a library board member. I served in a hospital authority and I was in the State Senate. I was Governor and I'm an engineer, naval officer, a farmer, a businessman. And I believe we require someone who can work harmoniously with the Congress, who can work closely with the people of this country and who can bring a new image and a new spirit to Washington.

Our tax structure is a disgrace and needs to be reformed. I was Governor of Georgia for four years. We never increased sales taxes or income tax or property tax. As a matter of fact, the year before I went out of office we gave a fifty-million-dollar refund for the property taxpayers of Georgia.

We spend six hundred dollars per person in this country—

every man, woman and child—for health care. We are fifteenth among all the nations of the world in infant mortality, and our cancer rate is higher than any country in the world. We don't have good health care. We could have it. Employment ought to be restored to our people. We've become almost a welfare state.

We spend now seven hundred percent more on unemployment compensation than we did eight years ago when the Republicans took over the White House. Our people want to go back to work.

Our education system can be improved.

Secrecy ought to be stripped away from government and a maximum of personal privacy ought to be maintained.

Our housing programs have gone bad. It used to be that the average family could own a house, but now less than a third of our people can afford to buy their own homes.

The budget was more grossly out of balance last year than ever before in the history of our country—sixty-five billion dollars—primarily because our people are not at work.

Inflation is robbing us, as we have already discussed, and the government bureaucracy is just a horrible mess.

This doesn't have to be.

I don't know all the answers—nobody could. But I do know that if the President of the United States and the Congress of the United States and the people of the United States said, "I believe our nation is greater than what we are now," I believe that if we are inspired, if we can achieve a degree of unity, if we can set our goals high enough and work toward recognized goals with industry and labor and agriculture along with government at all levels, that we can achieve great things.

We might have to do it slowly. There are no magic answers to it, but I believe together we can make great progress. We can correct our difficult mistakes and answer those very tough questions.

I believe in the greatness of our country, and I believe the American people are ready for a change in Washington. We've been drifting too long. We've been dormant too long. We've been discouraged too long and we have not set an example to our own people.

But I believe that we can now establish in the White House a good relationship with Congress, a good relationship with our people, set very high goals for our country, and with inspiration and hard work we can achieve great things and let the world know—that's very important—but more importantly, let the people in our own country realize that we still live in the greatest nation on earth.

Williamsburg, Virginia
October 22, 1976

Different People . . . Different Hopes . . . Different Dreams

I WANT to talk to you about some of my thoughts as I come to the end of a long political campaign.

The campaign began for me, as you know, some twenty-two months ago. I didn't have much money. Not many people knew who I was. I didn't hold public office. But I and my family campaigned for President just like you would if you wanted to be elected to the highest office in our country. In factory shift lines, barbershops, beauty parlors, livestock sales barns, farmers' markets, county courthouses, in the streets, shopping centers. Talking a little, listening a lot. And we learned about this country. There wasn't much media representation in those days. I was lonely. When I saw somebody with a scratch pad and a pencil or a microphone, I moved over their way and hoped they'd ask me a question. Most of the time they didn't.

But I learned. I learned about this country. And I understand the diversity of our nation much better than I did before. Our country is made up of pluralism, diversity. A lot of different kinds of people. But that's not a sign of weakness, it's a sign of strength. Some people have said that our nation is a melting pot. It's not. Whether we came to this country two years, twenty years, two hundred years ago—it doesn't matter. The point is why we came to this country. But when we come here, we haven't given up our individuality, our pride in our past history or background or commitments or habits. We become not a melting pot but a beautiful mosaic. Different people, different beliefs, different yearnings, different hopes, different dreams.

But all come together to make a beautiful picture of a common people. We came here because we wanted to. We came here because we believe in this country. We came here because we felt we could get along with one another even if sometimes we disagreed. And we haven't really been disappointed.

I've learned that this country faces great problems. I've met many college graduates who cannot find a job. I've met many men and women who have worked all their lives and then suddenly for reasons that they don't understand and which they cannot control were forced out of jobs and for the first time into the unemployment line. And later to draw their first welfare check. And that hurts a family when a man or woman, able to work, wanting to work, starts depending upon welfare. I've felt their anguish and I've experienced their embarrassment and I've talked to them quietly, and I've felt their shame when they lost their economic independence and their ability to care for their own families.

They became somebody's statistic. In the last two years since Mr. Nixon left office we've had two and a half million American families become unemployed. In the last two months alone, five hundred thousand Americans have become unemployed. And that hurts. I've met people who have been lucky enough to keep their jobs but have been driven to the brink of deprivation by runaway inflation. And . . . those who are still lucky enough to work, they are paying the bills, the welfare, unemployment compensation, and welfare costs. The ones who pay the bills are the ones who still have jobs.

I've met mothers and fathers who always felt sure in the past that they could buy a home. Nowadays, one of the most prevalent comments in our public opinion polls is "We can't plan anymore." Savings accounts that used to bring in a net profit now lose money, because the interest paid on the deposit doesn't equal the losses to inflation.

All this has hurt our nation. I've seen these problems and I've felt the frustration of people who sense that their problems are being caused not by themselves but by some remote bureaucrat in Washington and who feel and express to me quite often that "There's been a wall built around Washington we can't quite penetrate. Governor, we don't know how to make our expression of complaint or suggestion heard anymore."

There's been too much secrecy, and too little attention given to personal privacy.

I saw the disillusion of American people and so did you. With the assassination of John Kennedy and Bobby Kennedy and Martin Luther King, Jr., the shooting of George Wallace. There was a sense that somehow or other our societal structure was coming apart. And the scandals that hit our own government destroyed our core of stability and trust.

We've had a feeling that somehow the government that used to be our servant has become our master.

These are some of the impressions that I've gotten campaigning throughout the country in thirty primaries and since then in all fifty states. Either I or my family. But that's not all I saw.

I saw the underlying, unconquerable spirit of our people. I've seen the American people's courage, and I've seen the American people's hope. I've seen our determination not to surrender to setbacks and adversity, and I've seen our determination to get off of welfare and back to work.

I've seen in the midst of political scandal and corruption our determination to regain control of our governmental process and to restore to it competence, integrity, compassion, and unity. And also excellence. And greatness.

I've seen this determination and this courage, and I know that I shall never lose confidence in America, because American people have never lost confidence in themselves.

These are a few things that I've seen as I've run for President. And I've associated myself not with the despair but with the hope.

Not with the discouragement but with the optimism. Not with the negative aspects of life but with the affirmative commitment. Not with the past but with the future.

Because I know that these qualities that I've just described are what you yourselves have adopted in your own lives and hundreds of millions of Americans have adopted in their lives.

Tonight, almost on the eve of the election, an election that I do not intend to lose, I would like to look ahead with you for just a minute about what I see in the future.

I don't fear tough campaigns. Neither do you. I don't fear any close elections, and neither do you.

I have confidence in the American people's judgment, and so do you. I have confidence in the future of our nation, and so do you.

I see, on this two hundredth birthday celebration year of America, a new spirit. I see national pride restored. I see a revival of patriotism. I see an outpouring of a sense of volunteerism.

I see young Americans who don't drop out but are eager to help out, as they did in the early 1960s with the Peace Corps, before we were divided by war and assassinations and scandal.

I see the double standard of justice, where the average American is sent to prison and the big-shot crooks go free, abolished once and for all. I see everybody standing equal before the bar of justice.

I see an American government where economic policies are concerned with people and people's lives and people's families, not with abstract theories that are modified to a major degree by special interests who have inroads into the decision-making process and have carved out for themselves niches of privilege that the average American can never occupy....

That's the America that I want. That's the America you want. And this is the America that we can have if we'll work hard for the next six days and win this election and give the government of this country back to the people of this country.

Kennedy-Lawrence Dinner
Pittsburgh, Pennsylvania
October 27, 1976

News Conference

On Sunday, October 31, two days before the election, the Plains Baptist Church, of which Jimmy Carter is a lifelong member, canceled its services rather than admit a black political activist and minister from Albany, Georgia. This event was the day's top news story and caused some of Carter's supporters to fear it might cost him votes among the blacks and liberals, and possibly even cost him the election. Carter made a brief statement on the church closing on Sunday afternoon, then on Monday morning decided to hold a news conference to answer questions on it.

CARTER: Ten years ago, during the civil rights demonstrations, my family and I in our own church worked and tried to seek openness so that our church would receive anyone as a worshiper and a member without regard to race. In the interim period, our church has opened its door to anyone who's come there to worship. Recently, I think because of my presence in the church, as the Democratic nominee of our party, there's been a deliberate effort made to force the issue by someone who doesn't live in the community, who's a Republican, who's not a Baptist. And this has caused unfortunately a very serious problem to arise. The people in my home community, our pastor, our deacons, our church members, are trying to hold down the altercation so it wouldn't hurt my campaign—to be frank about it. And so it wouldn't divide our little church. . . .

My position now and then as a member of the church is that I intend to go home next Sunday and in subsequent worship services do what I can to ensure that there is not any discrimination in our church against anyone because they happen to be black or of any other race. And I could not be there this week. Perhaps if I had been there—I'm not a deacon anymore in our church—I could have had something to do with minimizing the problem. But this is something that I've had to face at a distance. None of my family is in Plains this week. As you know, we are campaigning all over the country. And I'm very deeply concerned about this and its impact on our little church and on possibly the campaign. But more because it shows that still within our country there is a remnant, sometimes a large remnant, of discrimination.

QUESTION: Governor, why don't you withdraw your own membership in that church, in opposition or as a protest to policies not acceptable to you?

CARTER: Well, the church, so far as I know, has never voted not to accept blacks into membership. In a Baptist church, the ultimate authority, the only authority, is the church membership. About ten years ago the church did vote, over my opposition and the opposition of my family, not to admit blacks and agitators. I think it was "colored" and agitators. Since then, though, when I was Governor of Georgia and since I've been a candidate for President, I have quite often gone to the church with black people and they have been welcomed into the church, as you have observed. I can't resign from the human race because there's discrimination. I can't resign as an American citizen because there's still discrimination. And I don't intend to resign from my own church because there's discrimination.

I think my best approach is to stay within the church and to try to change the attitudes which I abhor. Now if it was a country club, I would have quit. In fact, I have no membership in country clubs or any other private clubs that discriminate on account of race. But this is not my church, it's God's church. And I can't quit my lifetime of worship habit and commitment because of a remnant of discrimination which has been alleviated a great deal in the last ten years. I hope it will be eliminated completely in the next few weeks. I can't speak for the church membership. But I'll do all I can within the church to eliminate that last vestige of racial discrimination. ¹

Sacramento, California
November 1, 1976

You've Always Made Me Proud of You

At five P.M. on election day Carter spoke to several
thousand of his supporters in Plains before flying to
Atlanta to await the election results.

THANK YOU everybody. If there's anyone who has not yet
voted, you're excused to go vote and then come back.

I've been on the phone a lot today, talking to people
around the nation who report that in every part of our
country the voter turnout is tremendous.

And as you know, when this has happened in the primary
weeks, those long, sometimes lonesome, but always exciting
Tuesdays, we always come in on top, and I think we have a
good chance to come in on top tonight.

How many of you have been to another state to campaign
for me this year? I recognize you all around the crowd as I
came up the sidewalk. We've had five hundred or six hundred
Georgians, almost every day since the fall campaign began,
going as far away as Montana and New Mexico, and up into
Illinois—I know I shouldn't have started—Maine, New
Hampshire, Vermont. I think those are exciting trips and
ones that get a great deal of publicity and visibility, but it
means just as much to me, as you know, to have you here
in Plains, helping to run the headquarters and getting out
the vote in your own communities and around surrounding
states. This is the last day of a long effort on my part and on
your part which has been very exciting to me.

We haven't had any serious disappointments. I think, win
or lose tonight, and I think we have a good chance to win,
we've made political history, having come from a town the
size of Plains and not holding public office, just having my

wife and my sons and other members of my family and volunteers who campaigned all over the country.

We've never felt, nor have we acted, as though we were better than anyone else. We've put ourselves on the same plane, on the same level, with the same understanding as other hundreds of millions of Americans around this country. And you've added a great deal to the reputation and the image and the closeness that's been so rewarding to me politically. By letting others know that we have warm and open hearts, a sense of hope in times when many of us have been discouraged, and a sense that this country, in spite of serious disappointments in recent years, still has within its heart an inclination toward, and a capability for, excellence and greatness.

We know that our financial or political or economic or social status doesn't amount to much. What matters is what we are within ourselves, how well we can exemplify those virtues of unselfishness and dedication, patriotism, hope, a sense of brotherhood or sisterhood with our fellow human beings. And a vision of how we can make our lives better as free people in the greatest country on earth.

As we've been down through the long primary season, beginning the nineteenth of January with the caucuses in Iowa, and we surprised a lot of people, and in New Hampshire, the first primary, when we surprised a lot of people. Sometimes the same ones. And then quite often the same ones were surprised in Florida and the same ones were surprised in North Carolina and the same ones were surprised in Illinois and again in Wisconsin and Michigan and Ohio and Pennsylvania and many other states.

But I think the thing that has been the cause for the surprise has been the intense dedication and hard work of so many different people. Quite often the eyes of the television cameras and the attention of the newswriters were on me. But the campaign was being won by my family and by you.

This was kind of a secret weapon that we've had to bring us victories when quite often defeat was predicted for us.

I don't know what the voters will do today. This is the only poll that counts. I feel good about it, as you know. But I hope that sense of closeness among American people, spread from me to all of you and throughout the country, will be the basis for my own administration if I am the next President. You've never disappointed me. You've always made me proud. You've made me feel more rested when I was tired. And you've encouraged me when we've had temporary setbacks. And you've corrected me when I've made a mistake. But you've never lost faith in me. And I just want to be sure that when I am President that I'll serve in such a way that you'll never be disappointed, that you'll always be proud of me. That's my pledge to you.

I just want to make one more comment. We all want to win. And as I said earlier, we have an excellent chance to come in first. But no matter what the outcome of the election might be tonight, I hope that we don't lose our dedication and our high aspirations and goals and our love for one another and our pride in our own country. And if I should not be President, I hope that you will join with me in making our country great just the way we feel within our own hearts our country all ought to be.

But I think that because of your own help to me, and what we stand for and the humility that we can hope to maintain, that tonight when I come back to address many of you again, I'll come back as the President-elect of the United States.

Rally
Plains, Georgia
November 2, 1976

The Sun Is Rising on a Beautiful New Day

> At about seven A.M. on the morning after his election
> Carter returned to Plains to find that many of the sup-
> porters who had cheered him on his way the previous
> afternoon had waited all night for his return as President-
> elect. The sun rose just as Carter and his wife greeted
> the waiting crowd and both were visibly moved.

I CAME all the way through twenty-two months and I didn't
get choked up until I turned the corner and saw you standing
here. And I said, "People who are that foolish, we couldn't
get beat!"

The others, all the others who ran for President, didn't
have people helping them who would stay up all night in
Plains, Georgia, just to welcome me back.

I want to thank the band first of all; you've been up all
night. And the choir. It was a long night, but I guarantee
you it's going to be worth it to all of us.

It's been a good two years for us. I've learned a lot about
our country as you know. I've learned a lot about you, and
you've learned a lot about me. This campaign has drawn my
family closer together, and now I hope that I can be the kind
of President that will make this country as proud of me as I
am of you.

We've got a lot to learn still about one another. But there
is a need in this country for each individual person to look
deep within us and say, "What can we do to make our
country great? What can we do to make our future brighter?
What can we do to return laughter to the United States? And
hope?" And I believe that we are ready to do it.

This next couple of months I'll be doing the best I can to
prepare myself to be a President of whom all of you will be

proud. I believe that I can make the kind of leadership in the White House that can tap the greatness that's in all of you.

If we can just have a government—as I've said a thousand times—as good as our people are, that's all we could hope for and that's all we could expect and that's enough.

We're going to have a great government, a great nation, and it's because of you, not me.

I just want to say one more thing. I had the best organization any candidate ever had. Had the best family any candidate ever had. Had the best home community any candidate ever had. Had the best supporters in my home state any candidate ever had. And the only reason we were close last night was because the candidate wasn't quite good enough as a campaigner. But I'll make up for that when I'm President.

I guess you all know we're in it together. We'll just have to form a partnership with one another. I think it's going to be an enjoyable next four years. It's been an enjoyable last two years. And I believe that all of us will be proud that we were up all night last night and we meet here with the sun rising in the east.

I think the sun's rising on a beautiful new day. A beautiful new spirit in this country. A beautiful new commitment to the future. I feel good about it. And I love everyone of you and I thank you for it.

ROSALYNN CARTER: I just want to say thank you. You don't know how it is to be campaigning in the country, anywhere, and know that the people back home love you, care for you, are pulling for you, and it's just a good feeling. I'm glad to be home. Thanks, every one of you.

JIMMY CARTER: Now I think it's time for all of us to take one day off. Okay?

Rally
Plains, Georgia
November 3, 1976

4

Inaugural
Address

January 20, 1977

Inaugural Address

FOR MYSELF and for our nation, I want to thank my predecessor for all he has done to heal our land. In this outward and physical ceremony we attest once again to the inner and spiritual strength of our nation.

As my high school teacher, Miss Julia Coleman, used to say, "We must adjust to changing times and still hold to unchanging principles."

Here before me is the Bible used in the inauguration of our first President in 1789, and I have just taken the oath of office on the Bible my mother gave me just a few years ago, opened to a timeless admonition from the ancient prophet Micah:

"He hath showed thee, O man, what is good; and what doth the Lord require of thee but to do justly, and to love mercy, and to walk humbly with thy God." (Micah 6:8)

This inauguration ceremony marks a new beginning, a new dedication within our government, and a new spirit among us all. A President may sense and proclaim that new spirit, but only a people can provide it.

Two centuries ago our nation's birth was a milestone in the long quest for freedom, but the bold and brilliant dream which excited the founders of our nation still awaits its consummation. I have no new dream to set forth today, but rather urge a fresh faith in the old dream.

Ours was the first society openly to define itself in terms of both spirituality and human liberty. It is that unique self-definition which has given us an exceptional appeal— but it also imposes on us a special obligation, to take on those moral duties which, when assumed, seem invariably to be in our own best interests.

259

You have given me a great responsibility—to stay close to you, to be worthy of you, and to exemplify what you are. Let us create together a new national spirit of unity and trust. Your strength can compensate for my weakness, and your wisdom can help to minimize my mistakes.

Let us learn together and laugh together and work together and pray together, confident that in the end we will triumph together in the right.

The American dream endures. We must once again have faith in our country—and in one another. I believe America can be better. We can be even stronger than before.

Let our recent mistakes bring a resurgent commitment to the basic principles of our nation, for we know that if we despise our own government we have no future. We recall the special times when we have stood briefly, but magnificently, united; in those times no prize was beyond our grasp.

But we cannot dwell upon remembered glory. We cannot afford to drift. We reject the prospect of failure or mediocrity or an inferior quality of life for any person.

Our government must at the same time be both competent and compassionate.

We have already found a high degree of personal liberty, and we are now struggling to enhance equality of opportunity. Our commitment to human rights must be absolute, our laws fair, our natural beauty preserved; the powerful must not persecute the weak, and human dignity must be enhanced.

We have learned that "more" is not necessarily "better," that even our great nation has its recognized limits, and that we can neither answer all questions nor solve all problems. We cannot afford to do everything, nor can we afford to lack boldness as we meet the future. So together, in a spirit of individual sacrifice for the common good, we must simply do our best.

Our nation can be strong abroad only if it is strong at

home, and we know that the best way to enhance freedom in other lands is to demonstrate here that our democratic system is worthy of emulation.

To be true to ourselves, we must be true to others. We will not behave in foreign places so as to violate our rules and standards here at home, for we know that this trust which our nation earns is essential to our strength.

The world itself is now dominated by a new spirit. Peoples more numerous and more politically aware are craving and now demanding their place in the sun—not just for the benefit of their own physical condition, but for basic human rights.

The passion for freedom is on the rise. Tapping this new spirit, there can be no nobler nor more ambitious task for America to undertake on this day of a new beginning than to help shape a just and peaceful world that is truly humane.

We are a strong nation and we will maintain strength so sufficient that it need not be proven in combat—a quiet strength based not merely on the size of an arsenal but on the nobility of ideas.

We will be ever vigilant and never vulnerable, and we will fight our wars against poverty, ignorance, and injustice, for those are the enemies against which our forces can be honorably marshaled.

We are a proudly idealistic nation, but let no one confuse our idealism with weakness.

Because we are free we can never be indifferent to the fate of freedom elsewhere. Our moral sense dictates a clear-cut preference for those societies which share with us an abiding respect for individual human rights. We do not seek to intimidate, but it is clear that a world which others can dominate with impunity would be inhospitable to decency and a threat to the well-being of all people.

The world is still engaged in a massive armaments race designed to insure continuing equivalent strength among potential adversaries. We pledge perseverance and wisdom in our efforts to limit the world's armaments to those necessary for each nation's own domestic safety. We will move this year a step toward our ultimate goal—the elimination of all nuclear weapons from this earth.

We urge all other people to join us, for success can mean life instead of death.

Within us, the people of the United States, there is evident a serious and purposeful rekindling of confidence, and I join in the hope that when my time as your President has ended, people might say this about our nation:

That we had remembered the words of Micah and renewed our search for humility, mercy, and justice.

That we had torn down the barriers that separated those of different race and region and religion, and where there had been mistrust, built unity, with a respect for diversity.

That we had found productive work for those able to perform it.

That we had strengthened the American family, which is the basis of our society.

That we had insured respect for the law, and equal treatment under the law, for the weak and the powerful, for the rich and the poor.

And that we had enabled our people to be proud of their own Government once again.

I would hope that the nations of the world might say that we had built a lasting peace, based not on weapons of war but on international policies which reflect our own most precious values.

These are not just my goals. And they will not be my accomplishments but the affirmation of our nation's continuing moral strength and our belief in an undiminished, ever-expanding American dream.